MW00452633

The Norman Conquest

A Captivating Guide to the Normans and the Invasion of England by William the Conqueror, Including Events Such as the Battle of Stamford Bridge and the Battle of Hastings

© **Copyright 2019**

All Rights Reserved. No part of this book may be reproduced in any form without permission in writing from the author. Reviewers may quote brief passages in reviews.

Disclaimer: No part of this publication may be reproduced or transmitted in any form or by any means, mechanical or electronic, including photocopying or recording, or by any information storage and retrieval system, or transmitted by email without permission in writing from the publisher.

While all attempts have been made to verify the information provided in this publication, neither the author nor the publisher assumes any responsibility for errors, omissions or contrary interpretations of the subject matter herein.

This book is for entertainment purposes only. The views expressed are those of the author alone, and should not be taken as expert instruction or commands. The reader is responsible for his or her own actions.

Adherence to all applicable laws and regulations, including international, federal, state and local laws governing professional licensing, business practices, advertising and all other aspects of doing business in the US, Canada, UK or any other jurisdiction is the sole responsibility of the purchaser or reader.

Neither the author nor the publisher assumes any responsibility or liability whatsoever on the behalf of the purchaser or reader of these materials. Any perceived slight of any individual or organization is purely unintentional.

Free Bonus from Captivating History (Available for a Limited time)

Hi History Lovers!

Now you have a chance to join our exclusive history list so you can get your first history ebook for free as well as discounts and a potential to get more history books for free! Simply visit the link below to join.

Captivatinghistory.com/ebook

Also, make sure to follow us on Facebook, Twitter and Youtube by searching for Captivating History.

Contents

Introduction

There have been several key events throughout its history that have significantly altered the course of England. The first well-documented shift was when the Romans arrived and took control over the island, but they were hardly the last invaders to alter the path that the nation took. Following the departure of the Romans, the Vikings began to raid England's coasts, and, over time, they began to take control over parts of the island.

After the Romans' departure, the Anglo-Saxons remained in control of the island for several centuries, from 450 to 1066 CE. During this time, Viking leaders would occasionally take control over different parts of the island, but they were largely recorded as pretenders, and after their forcible removal, an Anglo-Saxon would become king again. The legendary King Arthur was based on one of the rulers who defended the island from the invasions of the Vikings.

However, the constant struggles continued well into the 11th century, and in part, they helped to destabilize the Anglo-Saxons. When the Anglo-Saxon King Æthelred II remarried after the death of his first wife, he chose the daughter of the Duke of Normandy, perhaps in the hopes of establishing some protection from the Vikings. However, his new wife, Emma, was not one to let go once she rose to power. When King Æthelred II died in 1016 and the Vikings again claimed the throne, she married the invader, King Cnut. Had her sons by this king survived, English history could have been even more different than it is today.

Because of the Vikings' successful invasion and Emma's refusal to let her line lose power, one of her sons by King Æthelred II would eventually inherit the throne. King Edward had little interest in ruling, or in anything secular, allowing the Godwinson family to have a lot more control over the kingdom's management than most kings would have allowed. When he died childless in early January 1066, the events of the last couple of decades left a large question over who was the rightful heir. While there was a legitimate heir to the throne (someone who was descended from King Æthelred II and his first wife), he was ignored as three men with less right to the throne fought over who would become king.

The year 1066 CE is one of the largest turning points in British history, with most people today having heard of the Battle of Hastings. The year had begun with the death of Edward the Confessor, a man who would be one of the last Anglo-Saxon kings. In the end, the course of the kingdom's history would shift as William the Bastard became William the Conqueror. He and his people would write their version of the history, meaning much of what we know today should be taken with a healthy dose of skepticism. Much like the "Histories" of Shakespeare are largely propaganda to improve the Tudor claim to the throne, William would ensure that history was recorded in favor of his lineage. Instead of recording events in the form of plays, the history based on William's perspective was recorded in the Bayeux Tapestry, a cloth tapestry that has as many as 75 scenes depicting the Norman invasion. The repercussions of his victory entirely changed the trajectory of the kingdom, as well as that of France.

Chapter 1 – England before the Death of a Pious King and the Norman Invasion

The island of Britain has an incredibly long history with numerous instances of invasions and the departures of those invaders. Each new conquering group of people brought with them the grains of the nation that would eventually form the nation of England. This has made it a nation that not only has a surprisingly diverse range in genetics for an island, but it also has had an effect on nearly every other aspect of England, especially the English language.

In the early days, the Romans were the first known invaders, and much of what is known today about England during that time period is from the Roman perspective. The next major group of invaders was the Vikings, who largely ended up settling down with the people who were already living there. The Vikings were less interested in recording history. While some details are known about the Anglo-Saxon period (with one of the most famous British legends—King

Arthur—being from this time), it is not as well documented as one would hope.

The Arrival and Departure of the Romans

Generally noted as the first major conquest of the people of the island, the Romans had marched across continental Europe and decided to continue their conquest beyond the continent. In 43 CE, they conquered the small island off the coast of what would one day be France. It was not the first time that the Romans had traveled across the channel. Julius Caesar had crossed the channel back in 55 BCE, which was met with the approval of the Roman people, although he had no interest in trying to conquer the island or its people.

This changed by 43 CE when Emperor Claudius decided that he wanted to expand the empire that Caesar had started. He sent Aulus Plautius to invade Britain, which the Romans were able to do with little difficulty in the southern parts of the island. But in other parts of the island, the remnants of the British tribes continued to attack the Romans until 51 CE when the Welsh chieftain Caractacus was captured. He was not just a fighter, though, and he befriended many powerful people. When Claudius held a parade to celebrate the victory in Britain, Caractacus was included in the procession. The Romans later recognized him for his courage, and he died in Rome.

Despite the loss of one of Britain's most notable chieftains, the Romans found that the unrest did not end. The leaders of the Celtic people, called the Druids, continued to resist the Romans for much of the Roman occupation. They were largely focused in modern-day Wales, so they did not pose a large threat to the majority of the conquering Roman soldiers. Despite this, there was relative peace for most of the Roman military, who were based on the island for roughly ten years.

When King Prasutagus, who ruled over a British Celtic tribe called the Iceni, died in 60 CE, his wife, Queen Boudica, was not willing to continue the peace. Not only had the Romans stolen their lands, but they had also sexually assaulted her daughters. As the leader of the Iceni, she allied her people with the Trinovantes, another Celtic tribe. Together, they attacked Londinium (modern-day London), Verulamium (modern-day St. Albans), and Camulodunum (modern-day Colchester). All of these Roman posts were burned. When Romans reinforcements returned, the reinforcements nearly wiped out all of her people. To ensure the Romans could not do anything else against her, she quickly committed suicide in either 60 or 61.

The Romans began pressing farther north and west between 70 and 90 CE. By the end of their expansion, they had established positions in Caerleon, Chester, and York. While they had some success against the people in what is now modern-day Scotland, they realized that they were being spread too thin. In 122 CE, Emperor Hadrian commissioned the construction of a large wall that still has remnants along the border with the Scots. When it was finished, Hadrian's Wall stretched for a little over seventy miles going from Newcastle to Carlisle, marking the regions that the Romans considered to be their territory on the island.

Following Hadrian's death in 138 CE, Emperor Antonius Pius decided to push north again with mixed results. He commissioned the construction of a new wall for the territories the Romans did take, naming it Antonine's Wall. By 160 CE, Hadrian's Wall had resumed being the border of the Roman Empire on the island, and the Romans continued to make further attempts to move farther north.

The people in the southern part of the island became accustomed to the Roman settlements. Many of the Roman laws and governmental structures were in place, and as a result, towns began to form in regions that had been more nomadic previously. The modern-day cities of Bath, Chester, Colchester, Gloucester, Lincoln, St. Albans, and York all have their roots during the Roman occupation. Native peoples could gain power by adopting Roman ways, which helped to establish an aristocracy on the island. The rest of the population saw little change in their daily lives during this time.

The decline of Roman power on the island took roughly 25 years from when it started to when they completely lost control of the nation. Trouble began not on the island but in western continental Europe, where the Germanic tribes were beginning to reclaim their lands from the Romans. The problems were largely internal in Rome as the people in power were increasingly less interested in the betterment of Rome and cared only for their own personal enrichment.

The revolt of Magnus Maximus, the commander of Britain, was the beginning of the decline of Roman control. Roman Emperor Gratian was wildly unpopular, and Maximus saw an opportunity to revolt against the Roman forces in Gaul around 383. He prepared his men in Wales and ensured that enough men were left to fight any potential Irish raiders who saw an opportunity to harm Wales while Maximus and his men were gone. He shuffled men around the island, taking control of the Roman forces for himself.

Ultimately, the way he reorganized the units removed some of the Roman bases, ending Roman rule there. From this point on, Rome did not directly control the island. Instead, it was controlled by men who were usually called usurpers by the Anglo-Saxons. Magnus Maximus left with his men, hoping to take control of the Roman Empire for himself. He failed, and no emperor after that was able to exert the same kind of control over the island.

The erosion of their power was finally seen as the Roman powers were forced off of the island in 409 CE. The Roman way of life began to decline on the island as the people began to reassert their own traditions and laws.

The Anglo-Saxons

The Anglo-Saxons were an established group who inhabited and ruled much of the island by the 5th century. The majority of Britain's population was mostly made up of people from the Germanic tribes of Angles, Jutes, and Saxons, and they had largely made peace with one another and the local inhabitants as they settled on the island. As they were so far from the continent, they were generally left alone during the Anglo-Saxon period, which ran from 410 CE to 1066 CE.

Institutions and regional governments were largely based in the new order that was created once the Romans were gone, and the use of Roman coins largely ceased. The towns that had formed under the Romans were largely abandoned, and the garrisons along Hadrian's Wall became bases for the local military and invaders. Without the Romans, the people were able to return to ruling themselves based on what worked best for their traditions.

By the later part of the 6th century, the Anglo-Saxon society had begun to form based on the people's values, with little influence from the Roman ways that remained in their new societies. Societies formed mainly based on region. Free peasants had control over their lands, and some began to coalesce into their own tribes and eventually kingdoms. Those who were the most successful warriors usually became kings of their small tribes and kingdoms.

One thing that was universal was the adoption of Christianity across the island and in Ireland. Ireland saw a much quicker coalescing of power under the religion. The Irish monk Columba was exiled (some say he exiled himself, while others say he was exiled by those in power) to Scotland in 565 CE for inciting and participating in violence that led to a civil war. He founded a spiritual movement that stretched well beyond the Emerald Isle and across modern-day Scotland and south into the northern parts of modern-day England. This was a period when knowledge thrived, and people sought more spiritual answers than power. The small kingdoms across both islands saw some struggles, but generally, societies and economies thrived under the more peaceful approach.

The later part of the 8th century and the beginning of the 9th century saw the growth of the Kingdom of Mercia. The political strength and influence that the kingdom had amassed over a couple of hundred years eventually become enviable for its power. Another powerful kingdom in England was also beginning to grow during the 9th century, Wessex. By the end of the century, Wessex was ruled by King Alfred the Great.

The power of these two kingdoms attracted the Norwegians in eastern continental Europe. That was when the Vikings began to raid the English coast.

The Repeated Attacks of the Vikings and the Rise of a Legend

Initially, Alfred did not seem like a candidate for the throne. He was the fifth son of King Æthelwulf of the West Saxons. As the fifth in line to the throne, he was largely left to pursue his own interests, which mostly revolved around learning and acquiring knowledge. This probably caused him to be less interested in becoming king, as being one would have limited how much time he could use to study and learn. Ironically, this is likely what made him such a great leader. The knowledge that he accumulated during his early years was probably the reason why he was able to accomplish so much, enough to be the basis for the legendary King Arthur. He was certainly one of the most notable rulers on the island.

As the son of a king, military strategy was certainly something he would be expected to know, even if he was not considered as a serious contender for the throne. By 868 CE, he was in active service in the military and joined King Æthelred I (his brother) in assisting King Burgred of Mercia against the Danish invasion. The Danes had arrived in East Anglia around 865 CE, and by 867 CE, they were in control of Northumbria. However, the Danish refused to fight, and a peace was negotiated. In 871 CE, the Danes again began to expand their grasp over the island, attacking Wessex. Alfred again joined his brother, and they engaged in several battles against the Danish forces. When Æthelred died that same year, Alfred was the next in line for the throne. However, he did not find success in his first battle against the Danes as the new king. The peace that followed the battle of Wilton did give the Danish invaders time to pause and consider their options. While the Danes had not failed in the battle, the West Saxon forces proved to offer more resistance than the Danes had anticipated. For the next five years, the Danish held off instigating any more battles against the new king.

In 876 CE, the Danes resumed their assault on the southwestern part of modern-day England. In 877 CE, they pulled back because they had accomplished very little with their skirmishes over roughly a year. Perhaps the five years that they had refrained from attacking Alfred and his military made them underestimate their opponent. It is also possible that during that time Alfred had spent more time ensuring that the military was ready for battle. Because the Danes had been so problematic throughout his entire life, there is little doubt that Alfred knew that they would try again to expand into his kingdom.

A third explanation could be that they wanted to gain the element of surprise. 878 CE had barely started when they attacked Wessex once more. During that initial push, they were able to take control of Chippenham, resulting in the majority of Alfred's forces relenting. It was said that all of the West Saxons submitted to the Danes with the exception of their king. Over the course of the next few weeks, he reminded the Danes of his presence through guerilla warfare. As he hounded the Danish with these random attacks, he also managed to assemble enough men to have a new army to support him less than two months after Easter. With his men, King Alfred defeated the Danes at the Battle of Edington. Following their surrender, the Danish king, Guthrum, agreed to be baptized into the Christian religion.

Following this last defeat of the Danes, Alfred was free to control the other aspects of his kingdom until 885 CE. It was at this point that the East Anglian Danes began to attack his kingdom. It took him a year, but in 886 CE, Alfred turned the tide and went on the offensive against this newest threat. When he was able to take what is now modern-day London, all of the English people who were not residing in Danish-held lands chose to acknowledge Alfred as their rightful king. Alfred may not have continued to press the Danish, but his son, Edward the Elder, was able to use the leverage that Alfred had gained by taking London to push farther into the Danish territories after he became king.

One of the primary reasons that Alfred did not continue to stretch his kingdom across the southern part of the island was because the Danish began to plan invasions from the continent. The new round of invasions lasted from 892 to 896 CE, in which Alfred proved that his successes in warfare were not a fluke. His ability to take defensive positions made it incredibly difficult for the Danish to gain any new ground. Any time Alfred had any available resources, he had old structures (particularly forts) strengthened, and then new ones were built in more strategic areas. He ensured that England's defensive posts were perpetually manned, leaving little chance for the Danes to launch a successful surprise attack. He started having his own ships built in 875 CE, so when new waves of invaders came, he was able to meet them and drive them back to the continent.

Nor was a secure defense his only military strength. Alfred understood that he needed the help of the other island kings, and he maintained a positive relationship with the rulers of Mercia and Wales. When they required assistance, he provided them with support, and they reciprocated when his people were under attack.

Beyond the Fighting

While he is famous for his military prowess, Alfred the Great was a capable leader in many other ways. As his interest lay more in traditional education and literature, he learned how to govern based on what other great rulers before him had done. He used the example of rulers like Charlemagne to restructure the different systems in the kingdom, such as the financial and justice systems, making them more efficient.

He was also intent on making sure that those in power did not exploit or oppress the weak or lower-class peoples of his kingdom. The practice of feuding, the practice of resolving a dispute between parties or families through a private war, was restricted (it could not be entirely banned as it was a part of the culture).

However, it was his reverence for learning that really set Alfred apart from other leaders. He believed that the Viking raids were a sign from the Christian god that people needed to repent for their sins. As long as they sinned, the Vikings would continue to attack. However, the lack of learning was part of the root cause of the problems, including the sins of the people. During the period of peace between 878 and 885 CE, he had scholars join him at court so that they could impart more knowledge and instruct him and others in Latin. He required all freemen who had time to learn to read English so that they could read the books that would give them useful and religious knowledge. Latin was largely only known among those in the Church. Alfred wanted his people to be able to read, so it made more sense for them to speak in their native tongue than to try to learn to read a language that they were largely only exposed to during religious ceremonies.

Although he was a very capable military leader, it was the changes that he made within the empire itself while keeping his people safe from repeated attacks that earned Alfred the epithet "the Great." More than just a knowledgeable military strategist, he was a humanitarian and sought to improve the lives of the people across England. He was remembered for centuries as the ideal king.

It is the society that he had established by the time of his death that had prepared the island for peace and prosperity. Smaller regions and principalities had been absorbed under him, and his kingdom was allied with the large kingdoms around them. The societies that grew out of his religious bent spread across most of Britain. It is the world as influenced by King Alfred that is generally considered the society of the Anglo-Saxons, and he remains one of the most renowned leaders, not only of their golden age but for all of British history.

Chapter 2 – Edward the Confessor and the Question of Succession

By the year 1066, England was a very different place than it had been at the beginning of the Anglo-Saxon period. However, that way of life was about to change significantly, and a new era was about to start on the island. This new period was initiated by another departure, but instead of removing a group of invaders, the people were about to experience a significant shift because of the death of their king.

King Edward the Confessor had lived a largely pious life, after having lived a very tumultuous life during his childhood and early adulthood. Given what had happened to him, it might have been expected that he would be more aware of how much trouble the nation could face if the king did not have an heir. Despite everything that he went through, though, Edward never had any children, largely owing to the tense relationship he had with his wife and her family.

When he died without any children, his kingdom faced one of the greatest problems it had seen since King Alfred's constant struggles against the Vikings. Unlike the earlier years of the Anglo-Saxon era, the kingdom was much larger, and the king was considerably more powerful than even King Alfred had been. Because of Edward's desire to focus on his spiritual life, England became engulfed in a civil war that changed the direction of the kingdom's future.

Edward's Life

Edward's desire to focus on the spiritual is understandable. Although he was the son of King Æthelred II and his wife, Emma of Normandy (the daughter of Richard I of Normandy), there was no guarantee that he would take the throne after his father's death. Edward's legitimate claim to the throne was threatened by the constant invasions by the Danes in 1013 CE, which caused the royal family to flee England and move to Normandy. Naturally, their apparent cowardice did not gain them friends among the English, and the English people were forced to face the invaders without their king.

The royal family took up residence in Normandy (part of modern-day northern France), where they lived in exile for a year. During this time, they planned how they would return to their kingdom and place their family in power once more. Edward accompanied several diplomats to England, where they negotiated the return of Æthelred II as king. This apparent good fortune did not last long as the newly restored king died in 1016.

Edmund Ironside would rule after Æthelred II's death from April until November 1016. During his incredibly short reign, he managed to put up a strong resistance to the Vikings led by King Cnut. His place in the line of succession was questionable as more support was given to the Viking king. Unfortunately for Edmund Ironside and those of Anglo-Saxon descent, he died soon after taking the throne. The cause of his death is not certain, but it is postured that he died of natural causes.

This unfortunate turn of events for the royal family was an opportunity for the Danes, who again returned to invade the island.

Without the king and the kind of support they needed, the queen and Edward returned to a life of exile in Normandy for several decades.

However, Queen Emma was not content to remain in exile. With her husband dead, she had a unique opportunity to give the invading Danish a legitimacy that they lacked to claim the throne—she could marry their king, Cnut. Together, they had another son and a daughter, who would one day become the queen of the German territories.

Naturally, the desertion of his mother did not sit well with the future king. Edward seemed to retain resentment against his mother for most of his life, although some historians have argued that she did the best she could under the circumstances. The children of King Æthelred II continued to live in exile while their mother lived with her new husband and their growing family in England. Edward did not marry while he was in exile, choosing to spend more time hunting and acting like a nobleman than in looking for a resolution of the problem against his mother and her new family. His life was largely mundane until 1035, which was when his stepfather, Cnut, died.

At the time of Cnut's death in England, his son with Emma, Harthacnut, was occupied with conducting a war against Magnus I of Norway. Cnut had collected a number of lands during his time as king, including England, Denmark, Norway, and some of Sweden, lands that his son was trying to maintain within a single kingdom—a task that he failed to achieve. With the king dead and the prince (who became king of Denmark after his father's death) abroad fighting another war, Emma was forced to face the reality that the son she had doted on was not likely to get the throne because the British people preferred her stepson, Harold Harefoot, who was the son of Cnut. Faced with the possibility of her lineage being removed from the throne, Emma finally turned to the children whom she had left in exile when she returned to power in England. Both Edward and his brother, Alfred **Ætheling**, returned to England. They both became entangled in battles, and Harold Harefoot captured and killed Alfred in 1036.

Emma waited for her son Harthacnut to return to her so that they could remove Harold from power. Having escaped from England after his return there, Edward claimed to have no interest in the throne. That left Harthacnut as Emma's only way of carrying on her family's line as the rulers of the kingdom.

Harthacnut was working to create a larger fleet (he only had ten ships when he landed in Flanders in 1039), but before he had a chance to attack his half-brother, Harold died in early 1040. Emma and Harthacnut returned to England to reclaim the throne that they had a better claim over the last remaining son of the late King Æthelred II. Cnut was seen as a usurper, and Emma was only queen through marriage, not by blood. Though Harthacnut was Emma's favorite child, both he and the queen extended an invitation for Edward to join them in England, where he would rule as a joint king.

Edward's claim to the throne was actually stronger, as he was the only living son of King Æthelred II, but he had spent most of his life living abroad. Despite having said he was not interested in ruling, Edward did return and worked alongside his half-brother to rule the kingdom. In 1042, Edward found himself in a completely different situation following the death of Harthacnut. Just like Harold, Harthacnut did not have any children, leaving the nation in turmoil as people tried to decide who would next sit on the throne. Harthacnut had a cousin named Sweyn Estridsson who considered himself to be the rightful heir, and there were others who were mentioned as being potential kings, such as Magnus I of Norway—the man that Harthacnut had been fighting when his father died and the man that became king of Denmark when Harthacnut died. Rumors said that Emma had considered Magnus, but ultimately, she supported Edward.

By this time, Edward, who was 39 years old, was already older than most Anglo-Saxon kings had been when they died. Edward went on to give England more than two decades of stable rule, and the nation prospered as a result. The early years of his reign were tumultuous as some claimants felt they had a better right to the throne, and he was largely a stranger to everyone in England, after having spent about a quarter of a century living in exile. His biggest opponent was the one who had initially supported him—his mother, Emma.

Despite the fact that Edward had a better claim to the throne than most other possible candidates, Emma (who had a long history of scheming against the kings with Godwin, Earl of Wessex) plotted against her son, in part because she wanted to retain control of England as queen. Her frequent co-conspirator, Godwin, retained considerable power and ruled in all but name for eleven years. Edward appeared to be content with the arrangement in the beginning, having spent much of his life far from London. Godwin had the support of the people, and Edward was aware that he was not as popular or commanding as the man who had lived in England through decades of unrest.

In 1045, Edward married Godwin's daughter, Edith, to give the powerful man a blood relation closer to the throne. However, the king and the shadow king did not always agree on issues and resolutions. In 1049, they had irreconcilable differences, and Edward began to take a larger role in the governing of the realm. Two years later, he declared the Godwin family outlaws, including his own wife. Unfortunately, for the king, his reliance on and favoritism shown to foreigners quickly lost him the goodwill of the people. When Godwin returned in 1052 with his sons and an army, the English people were willing to support him. Edward retained his position as king, but he had to take his wife back and restore all of the Godwin lands to the family.

The following year, 1053, Godwin died, and his son, Harold Godwinson, began to take the place of his father, particularly when it came to keeping the approval of the people. There was one way that Edward could keep his brother-in-law in line, and that was through dangling the throne as a potential option. As Edward had no heirs and had no inclination to have them, it was a tactic that he successfully used for over two decades to keep people loyal to him.

Promises about Succession

For years, it is said that Edward held the promise of the line of succession out to people to get what he wanted or needed, but Harold was essentially a shadow king after his father died. With no clear successor to the throne, it certainly was a very powerful bargaining chip for a man who was not popular with the people he ruled. Queen Elizabeth I would do something similar several centuries later when she became queen and was still unmarried (the primary difference being that she was incredibly popular with the people).

Harold proved that he was a capable leader, even before Edward died, as he finally forced Wales to submit to English rule and also negotiated a peace with the Northumbrians. All of this he did between 1063 and 1065. However, he managed to ostracize his brother, Tostig, who would later side against him when the Vikings invaded.

Despite his strength as a leader, the person with a claim to the throne through actual blood relations was William, the Duke of Normandy, more commonly known in history as William the Conqueror. As Edward's distant cousin, he had a much stronger claim to the throne in terms of blood, and some historians believe that Edward actually promised the throne to William. Though Harold was popular with the people, he was not a blood relation to the royal family, and there was no chance that his sister would ever make the connection valid. Edward had taken her back as his wife because he had been forced to; that did not mean that he felt compelled to further his own line. With the capable William as a potential successor, Edward likely felt that the best solution was to pass the throne on to someone who was capable and had already been through similar hardships as himself. Or perhaps he felt that this was the best way to get back at the family who had forced so much on him after trying to remove him from the throne, attempts that were backed by his own mother.

However, it is also possible that he chose Harold as the next king because Edward knew that Harold had the support of the people. Essentially, the Godwin family had been ruling the country in all but name since Edward had been restored to the throne. Harold was not only popular; he had grown up in the country and had much stronger ties to England than William. Having been unpopular because he had spent much of his life in exile and was not familiar with the customs or traditions like the Godwin family, it is possible that Edward actually did believe that Harold was the best suited to rule the people. William had not lived in the country, which made him less likely to take the best interests of the people in mind. He also had gained a reputation for being brutal and merciless, two things that Edward the Confessor would almost certainly have detested in a leader. The Godwins may have given Edward problems, but they had also allowed the king to be largely left to his own devices, focusing on the spiritual instead of the day-to-day workings of the kingdom. And the country had prospered because of it.

Considering how poorly his mother had treated him over the course of his life, it is difficult to blame Edward for not having children, but he definitely should have made it clear who was to take the throne when he died. Instead, people were left to believe the words of those who had been with him in his final moments.

Edward's Death and the Island on Edge

When he was dying, Edward finally gave his decision as to who he wanted as his successor. According to those who had been with him as he was dying, the king named Harold to be his successor. After everything that had happened during his life, Edward should have known how much people would contest anything that was said from his deathbed. For someone who was said to be pious, Edward had to be aware that his years of dangling the succession in front of others was going to cause infighting because all of these people had been led to believe that they had a chance of being king. That does not even account for the people who felt they had a claim once the childless king died.

Edward's childless marriage later came to be seen as a sign of just how pious he was, earning him sainthood and the name Edward the Confessor. Naturally, this overlooks the problems that his childlessness actually did cause for England. The fact that he didn't have children also was not likely a result of his piousness, though it is not certain why he didn't have children. It could have been a disinterest in having a family after what he had experienced, or he simply didn't want another distraction from what he felt was important. In contrast to those who feel his life mirrored his angelic nature, some believe he was an ineffective ruler, while others believe that he was shrewd and knew his own limitations. As king, the only power that he insisted on retaining was in naming the bishops of the Church; most of the other powers of his position were exercised by Godwin and his son for most of Edward's reign. Although he had accepted the throne, Edward proved that he had not been entirely untruthful when he said he did not want it. His only real interest was in ensuring that the Church had the support that it needed.

This is why it is possible that he actually did leave the kingdom to Harold. Even though Edward had not wanted to have the Godwin family restored to power, they were placed back in power in all but name anyway. Godwin and his son did all of the things that Edward did not want to do, as he did not feel that those roles were important. While he was pushing to have a better, more enlightened Church, the Godwins helped the nation to prosper, creating a stable life for the people of England.

When Edward died, he left a power vacuum that would not be resolved peacefully. The new king, Harold Godwinson, reigning as Harold II, was crowned the next day, but that did not resolve the question of who the rightful heir to the throne was. Edward had all but ensured that the question of succession would only be settled through war.

When Edward died on January 5th, 1066, it was just a matter of time before those who felt that they had a claim to the throne came forward, shattering the security that the kingdom had known under Edward and the shadow king Harold. Though there is definitely a lot of doubt cast on who he left the throne to, it is not likely that Edward actually left it to William. Harold and his wife were already at hand, whereas William resided in Normandy, across the English Channel. Harold knew the inner workings of being king since he had been doing it for years. Logically, Harold made the most sense. While it meant the kingdom would be passing out of the hands of his lineage, Edward could have been ensuring that the nation continued to be ruled by an Anglo-Saxon. William was decidedly not one of them, and with his reputation, it is difficult to imagine Edward actually naming him as the kingdom's successor. Or perhaps Edward was largely indifferent because he did not care for the position himself.

Chapter 3 – The Norwegian King Harald Hardrada

There were a number of people who sought to follow Edward the Confessor as the English king, but none of them had quite the blood claim that William of Normandy had. The majority of those who wanted to rule the island only had claims based on the usurpers who had taken it from the native people.

The man who had been given the crown, Harold Godwinson, was not only a member of the English nobility, but he also had a lot of support from the people of England. He and his father had long held considerable power, and he was favored over many of the people who had decided to try to lay a claim to the throne. The fact that he was not related by blood was not seen as a problem by many of the Anglo-Saxons. King Harald, on the other hand, had no claim based on blood or right of succession. His interest was largely in expanding to the island that had prospered so well under the Godwin family.

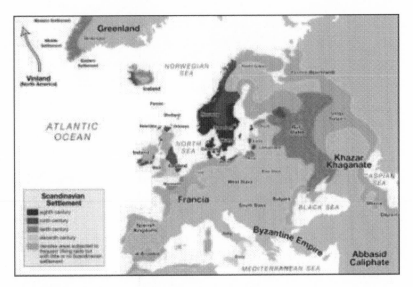

Viking Raids and Settlements up to 1066

(*Source:*
https://www.ducksters.com/history/middle_ages_viking_expansion.jp
g)

King Harald Hardrada's Life before Invading England

Harald Sigurdsson, who later earned the well-known epithet "Hardrada," meaning hard ruler, was the son of one of the major Norwegian chieftains, a renowned Viking named Sigurd Syr. The family claimed to have been descended from the first king of Norway named Harald Fairhair, although the claim may have been made following Hardrada's death so that his actions would be considered legitimate. Olaf, his half-brother, had been chosen by five minor chieftains to be the king of Norway.

When King Cnut took the throne of Denmark in 1029 CE, Olaf and Harald resisted. The disputes between the families resulted in Olaf being exiled, but he did not stay away for long. In 1030, Olaf returned to Norway, and he and his forces were planning to remove Cnut from his position as king. Harald was staunchly on Olaf's side, and they fought Cnut in the Battle of Stiklestad, where Olaf was killed. Only sixteen years old during that battle, Harald was largely untested as a warrior. He made it out of the battle with his life, but he sustained injuries and was exiled for his participation in the insurrection against the king.

He spent many of the succeeding years in exile, during which time he gained the military experience he needed to try to remove the king again. He spent time in part of modern-day Russia and gained the necessary battle experience against adversaries who were less organized than the men under King Cnut. Harald made a name for himself as a capable warrior, and he was able to attract a band of a few hundred men to fight under him.

With his experienced men, Harald went to the capital of the Byzantine Empire, Constantinople, in roughly 1034. Although they were Vikings, important people of the empire took notice of them, and they were soon hired to be a part of the renowned Varangian Guard. The primary responsibility of the Varangian Guard was to protect the emperor. During his time working as a member of the elite fighters, Harald traveled into much of the world that would have been considered exotic where he came from, such as modern-day Iraq. They went with the negotiators from the Byzantine Empire to Jerusalem, as well as fighting against a range of other enemies on the Mediterranean Sea. This gave him the experience he needed in fighting on water and having to plan for other, less familiar methods of fighting.

By 1041, the politics of the empire had changed, and the Byzantine emperor that Harald and his men had served was dead. As Michael V and Empress Zoë vied for power, Harald went out of favor, perhaps because he supported the former empress, even after Michael V had been given control over the empire. Harald was subsequently imprisoned, though the reason for it has been obscured. Several reasons have come down over the centuries, including an accusation of defrauding the emperor, murder, and defiling a noblewoman. Given the large differences in potential reasons, it is most likely that Michael V and his allies were simply looking to neutralize Harald. The prison could not contain him, though, and upon his escape, Harald rejoined the Varangian Guard to fight against the new emperor. They were successful, and Michael V was removed from power.

It did not take a year before he was again out of favor with Empress Zoë. Realizing that his time in Constantinople was up, he left before he could again be accused of further crimes. However, Empress Zoë rejected his request to leave the Varangian Guard. Harald did not stick around, slipping out of the Byzantine Empire with those men who chose to leave with him. They took control of two ships, losing one to the iron chains in the strait (an obstacle placed across navigable waters to prevent ships from using the waters). After his time fighting the Muslims and other enemies of the empire, Harald knew how the Byzantines would try to catch him, and a mixture of luck and skill helped him escape and finally return to Kievan Rus' in 1042.

During his time away from his people, Harald had accumulated a lot of wealth, most of which he brought with him. Over time, he had sent the wealth that he gathered to the Grand Prince Yaroslav I (known as Yaroslav the Wise), the leader of the people Harald had helped after the death of Olaf, for safekeeping. Having once failed to woo the leader's daughter, Harald was successful the second time around. Yaroslav allowed the marriage, despite Harald's lack of title or claims to the Kievan Rus' throne.

Deciding it was time to return to his native lands of Norway, Harald packed up his riches and new wife and went to try to reclaim the throne. Upon his arrival, he found the royalty to be totally different than when he had left. King Cnut had died in England, and his eldest sons had likewise perished during Harald's absence. The bastard son of his half-brother Olaf, Magnus I, or Magnus the Good, had ascended to the throne, putting the lands back in his family's bloodline. Despite having supported Olaf, in 1046, Harald decided to challenge his nephew for the throne. To bolster his forces, he allied with Anund Jacob, the king of Sweden, who also felt that he had the right to take the Norwegian throne. They also allied with Sweyn Estridsson, Harthacnut's cousin, who had a much lesser claim to the throne.

Together, the three leaders raided all along the Danish coast, harassing Magnus with the traditional lightning-quick strikes for which the Vikings are still infamous. Seeing that this was not only harming his people but also making him less popular, Magnus' advisors pushed for the king of Norway and Denmark to split control with the battle-hardened Harald. His uncle would be allowed to take the throne of Norway, ruling the people under Magnus, who would retain the throne of Denmark. Harald would have to agree to Magnus being the overlord of the two countries, but he would be allowed to largely manage Norway as he saw fit. Harald agreed, and the two established their own courts and power within their respective countries, rarely meeting to discuss the affairs of their nations.

This arrangement did not last long as Magnus died in 1047, and he had no sons (legitimate or illegitimate) to rule after him. He had not wanted Harald to succeed him, so before his death, Magnus the Good named Sweyn Estridsson to be his successor. This was certainly ironic as Magnus had beaten Sweyn while Harald was off fighting for the empire, and Sweyn had allied with Harald against Magnus upon Harald's return to the region.

How prepared Sweyn was for the inevitable attack by Harald is unclear, but Harald definitely made the first move to try to restore the two kingdoms under one ruler. Instead of invading Denmark in a major assault, Harald opted to use the same tactics he and Sweyn had used against Magnus. The lightning raids along the Danish coast proved to be far less effective as Sweyn did not budge when the same tactics were used against him.

This struggle to combine the two nations under one king resulted in fifteen years of war, and the two leaders were finally forced to face off at the Battle of Niså in early August 1062. With the knowledge of far more diverse and foreign attacks at his disposal (thanks to his time working for the empire), Harald emerged victorious, though it did not accomplish what he had wanted. Sweyn fled the battle with many of his close advisors and most trusted men. Sweyn did not have the military prowess that Harald had, but he also knew that and had no problem fleeing when the odds were stacked against him. Harald and Sweyn continued to fight for another three years before Harald finally opted for peace. In 1065, Harald finally made a truce with the Danish king.

By this time, Harald was fifty years old. Having started fighting for control of Norway when he was just sixteen years old, fighting was one of the things that Harald understood best. With a truce in place with Sweyn, the Norwegian king became restless and decided to turn his attentions elsewhere. The obvious target for his attention was the riches of Britain, a land that the Vikings had targeted for roughly the last two and a half centuries. If he could bring England into his realm, as King Cnut had done, Harald felt that he would finally have a large kingdom to control and a way to ensure that his name went down in history.

King Harald's Claim to the Throne

Of all those laying claim to be the next king of England, King Harald had the weakest claim, even according to the Viking rules. King Cnut had ruled all of Denmark and Norway before taking on England. The line of succession would have meant that the ruler of all the continental kingdoms would also rule England, something that Harald had failed to achieve. The kingdom was fractured in large part because of Harald.

More importantly, the Anglo-Saxons did not recognize King Cnut as a legitimate king. To them, he had been a pretender. There was no point where they would have wanted another Viking on the throne, so even if King Harald had successfully taken the continental part of the old kingdom back, he would not have been recognized as legitimate to the people of the island.

Chapter 4 – William, Duke of Normandy

Before he became known as William the Conqueror, the man who would one day be the king of England was known as William the Bastard. This was both an identification of the situation of his birth and the reputation he had gained over the years as he grew up in Normandy. It is also possibly true that because of his illegitimate status, he felt that he had to prove himself and be tougher than the legitimate sons of Robert I. However, his desire for power was typically on full display as William eventually began to threaten the French king, Henry I. His distant kinship to Edward the Confessor (a first cousin once removed) and a claim that Harold Godwinson had promised to support him (several years before Edward's death) would be his primary reasons for seeking to bring England under his control.

Robert I of Normandy

William was born to Duke Robert I of Normandy and Herleva, his mistress, who was better known as Arletta. While William's father was a member of the nobility, his mother was just the daughter of a tanner with no noble blood. William's maternal grandfather was a successful merchant who had accumulated enough wealth to attract the attention of the members of the nobility. Herleva and Duke Robert I of Normandy did not stay together, and she would eventually marry Herluin de Conteville and have two sons with her husband, giving William two half-siblings.

William's father, Duke Robert I of Normandy, was known by two names: Robert le Magnifique (Robert the Magnificent) to his friends and family, and Robert le Diable (Robert the Devil) to his enemies. He also had a claim to the English throne as he was the great-grandson of Richard I of Normandy (father to Emma, Edward's mother). Upon his father's death, Robert fought with his brother, Richard III of Normandy, about who would control Normandy. Richard III was the elder son, which gave him a better claim to take over the region. However, Richard III died not too long after taking control, and upon his death, Robert I took over the rule of Normandy. With Normandy finally under his control, Robert quickly decided that it was not enough.

Robert I proved to be a fairly demanding ruler and a horrible neighbor, as he claimed lands from various fiefdoms around him and from the Church. He bullied lesser aristocrats, taking their lands and demanding their allegiance. All of this meant that after his brother's death, Robert I had more influence than when he had initially contested Richard III's claim to the throne. Soon, Robert II of France, also known as Robert the Pious, died in 1031. Robert I had been living in Normandy, and with his large power base, he decided to back Henry I of France for the throne. Robert I of Normandy died without any legitimate heirs in 1035 CE.

William's Early Life

Born in 1027 or 1028, William's illegitimacy was not as detrimental to his status as it was to families with less status or wealth; however, it should have excluded him as the heir to Normandy. With wealth on one side and power on the other, he was always going to have a fairly easy time in life, even if he should not have been able to take over his father's lands. William had two half-brothers, Odo of Bayeux (who became the bishop of Bayeux) and Robert, Count of Mortain (who became the earl of Kent), after his mother married. They would prove to be very helpful to him as they always supported him in his endeavors.

After Robert I of Normandy died while on a pilgrimage to Jerusalem, the wheels of the plans he had put in place to ensure his bloodline continued were tested. Knowing that he had no other heirs, Robert I had taken some steps to ensure that his lineage would continue to rule after his death. To guarantee that his lineage would be recognized through his illegitimate son, he had his barons take an oath of loyalty to William. The problem was that without Robert I around, there was no guarantee that his wishes would be respected (a problem that his line would later face in England).

With so much power having been accumulated during Robert I's reign, the people needed someone to take control and help the region to prosper as quickly as possible. Though he was an illegitimate son, William was the most obvious choice. Despite the circumstances of his birth, the nobles honored their oaths to support William as the new duke, and he was quickly recognized as the next successor to the dukedom. It did mean ignoring the rules since a child born out of wedlock meant that a person could never inherit or lay claim to any power that their parents had.

The major problem, though, was that he was only around seven years old. For the next two years, the Duchy of Normandy was managed by William's great uncle, Gilbert, Count of Brionne. The problems of the region were already beginning to simmer, though, and without the tough Duke Robert I in control, the nobles began to rebel. This resulted in a civil war within Normandy, and Gilbert was killed. Though he was still young, William did have a number of powerful relatives and supporters, such as the archbishop of Rouen, who was his uncle Mauger, and Herluin de Conteville (his stepfather). Henry I of France helped him to put down the dukes trying to cut into his territories because the civil war was threatening to damage trade in France, as one of the main trade routes ran through Normandy.

When William turned fifteen years old, the French king, Henry I, knighted him. From that point on, William was largely on his own to take care of Normandy, though he did have help when he needed it. However, King Henry I did not remain as one of his allies. In 1047, problems related to William's rising power finally became more apparent as regions around Normandy had become unstable. Seeing such a young child on the throne had made those around Normandy decide that it was now the time to start trying to chip away at the powerful dukedom. It is clear why William developed such a hardline against others as he had been fighting to keep his dukedom intact since he was a young child. He saw some of his relatives killed as they tried to aid him, and some of his former supporters turned on him. After he finally ended the rebellions, William began to seek to expand his own empire. For twenty years, he demonstrated that the circumstances of his youth had proven to be highly effective in teaching him how to best strategize against his enemies. He became so efficient at consolidating his power that he disrupted the power balance in France.

To this day, he is known as one of the most formidable strategists and military commanders of the Middle Ages. Most people today have heard one or both of his names (William the Bastard and William the Conqueror), even if they are not entirely sure who he is or why he is still known today. His reputation began long before he reached the shores of England because of the turmoil that he experienced at such a young age.

Rebellions within the region were problematic, but King Henry I of France also turned against him in 1054 and attacked William. Over time, William had terrorized and bullied people into ensuring things went his way. Frequently attacking Flanders and Anjou, William became one of the most powerful men in France, making Henry I very uncomfortable. King Henry I feared the unrivaled power William had gained by upsetting or intimidating the majority of

France, as he had either taken control of many different regions or strategically had marriages arranged between his nobles and his rivals. Ultimately, he became the most powerful man in France.

William not only put down the rebellions within Normandy, but he and his forces also defeated King Henry I at the Battle of Mortemer in 1054. This did not end the contention between them, though, as Henry I again attacked in 1057. The Battle at Varaville during that year nearly saw the death of the king, who had to flee from the capital. Henry I found himself and about half of his army on one side of the river, having barely escaped William and his men. All the king and his forces, those who had managed to escape, could do was watch as the floodwaters of the river rose, and the men who could not escape across the river were slaughtered by William's army.

When Henry I died in 1060, his son, Philip I, took over the throne. Just like William had been, Philip I was too young to actually rule the nation. The new king's guardian was Baldwin V of Flanders, who, by this time, was William's father-in-law. Philip I was only seven years old when he became king, and it was his mother, Anne of Kiev, who served as regent until he turned fourteen years old.

With such a young king on the throne, whose advisor and mother were not interested in continuing to fight, there was no longer any reason for the king and William to fight. These familial bonds were something that he had learned to wield to great effect, and this was just one more example of how William managed to resolve an issue without fighting. He is remembered for his military prowess, but his ability to forge alliances through marriage was just as strategic.

No longer having to worry about retaining his power in Normandy, William took this opportunity to finally take stock of his situation. Without a king who feared his power, William decided that he could continue his expansion, but it would mean focusing on somewhere new. As a distant relation to the king of England, it was clear to him where he should turn his attention next.

The problem was that, technically, he was a vassal to the French king. As a vassal, he could not attack another country without first trying to find a peaceful resolution. That meant that he would have to start with diplomacy, something that he had mastered nearly as well as military strategy. However, William knew that the likelihood of success was slim.

There was a second issue that would prove to be problematic, at least initially. France and England had some ties, but they largely had not attacked each other over the years. There was no obvious benefit of taking the English throne to the members of his nobility. He had to convince them that it would be worth the preparation and struggles to take the kingdom that had proven to be their equals in battle. This ended up being less complicated than William may have initially believed, as the promise of new lands and titles that would go to those who supported the venture persuaded a large number of the French nobility to join him.

His Claim to the Throne

By 1066, the fighting that had plagued Normandy because of the contention between William and the French King Henry I was over, and the new ruler of France allied with him to face the king of England. William's ostracization because of the status of his birth also drove him to seek additional approval, so he went to the pope. After receiving papal approval, he had everything in place to lay his claim to the English throne.

It was certainly true that William was related to Edward the Confessor. They were both related to Count Richard I of Normandy; Count Richard I of Normandy was Edward's grandfather and William's great-grandfather. They were distant relations, but William was a closer relation than Harold, whose sister had been married to Edward the Confessor. This logic was what had won William the support of so many.

Despite this, William had spread word that Edward had promised him the throne and that Harold Godwinson had pledged his allegiance to William during a visit to Normandy in 1064 CE. It was possible that this happened, as Harold had been in Normandy some years earlier. However, it is by no means certain that this actually happened. And if it did, it is possible that William had forced the oath out of him, meaning it was done against Harold's will.

William claimed that Edward had promised that he would be the heir back in 1051 when he went to visit England. While this is possible, Edward the Confessor did use this kind of promise to keep people in check, so whether or not he had meant it (if he had even made the promise in the first place) is not without a lot of doubt. During 1051, the Godwin family had been exiled from England, so it is possible that in his anger, Edward had promised the throne to William, though even that could have been to keep William from attacking while Edward was at his most vulnerable.

According to the Anglo-Saxons, Edward promising the throne to William was a lie to justify his actions. But despite England's protests, other kings sided with William. It was likely that they would have supported him regardless, as the idea of a throne going to someone who was not a blood relation to a ruler could have established a dangerous precedent. When Harold II of England refused to give up the throne, despite the decree of the pope, William had all of the justification that he needed to invade England. As King Harald Hardrada marched on the island without any backing by the rest of the continent, William began his preparations to attack the newly crowned king, Harold II, himself. Beginning in the summer of 1066, William found himself planning how to cross the English Channel and what the best strategy would be to expand his power into England. He did not have to worry too much about Normandy and the lands that he had taken because his connections within France and his reputation would keep his lands safe.

It is interesting to note that the pope had done more than just back William; he had also excommunicated Harold II. It is possible that

Harold II did not take this well, and some say that he may have been disheartened by this apparent betrayal. Still, Harold did not relent in his claim, foreshadowing the events that would happen several centuries later under Henry VIII, who managed to finally break free from the Catholic Church.

Chapter 5 – Harold II of England

Perhaps the strongest claim to the English throne actually lay with the man who was coronated the day after Edward died, Harold Godwinson. His father had been integral in running the country and had worked with Edward the Confessor since he first became king. After his death, Harold took his father's place managing the secular aspects of the kingdom. His family may not have been related to the throne by blood, but they were a noble Anglo-Saxon family.

Early Life

Born in the early 1020s (usually estimated around 1022), Harold was the son of the Earl of Wessex, Godwin. The family was of noble Anglo-Saxon heritage that had been a part of the development of the nation for centuries, a tradition that had been strengthened under Edward the Confessor. Harold's mother, Gytha Thorkelsdóttir, had links to the Danish throne; her brother, Ulf Thorgilsson, had married Cnut's sister, Estrid. Harold had seven siblings, including Edith, the sister who married King Edward. His brothers were given their own regions to manage, though things did not always go smoothly between Harold and his brothers.

When he was still in his early 20s, Harold was given the title of earl of East Anglia, giving him a large estate to control. During the beginning of the 1050s, Harold and his family became entangled in disagreements with King Edward, and the family members had to flee the country for a while, including Queen Edith. After leaving their lands, members of the Godwin family spent time in Ireland. Edward quickly learned just how little power he actually had without the powerful Godwins helping him. When he had been living in Normandy during his exile and the kingdom was under control by Cnut, the Godwin family had remained in England. Without the Godwins, Edward's grasp over his kingdom was tentative, and in addition, he now had to take care of the aspects of ruling that he had no interest in managing. The family had left in 1051, but they returned to their lands in 1052.

Following Godwin's death in 1053, Harold inherited the title of the earl of Wessex. Because of the new title, Harold was not allowed to keep his former title of earl of East Anglia because of the power imbalance it would have created between the earls of the kingdom. Edward the Confessor was the one who ordered Harold to give up his first earldom, but despite this, Harold was still the most powerful earl in England, and it could be argued the most powerful person in the kingdom, as Edward had allowed his father to largely run the country and continued to allow Harold to do so as well.

Internal Strife

During his time in assisting Edward the Confessor, Harold had been required to manage uprisings and problems within the kingdom. In 1063, he successfully attacked the king of Wales, Gruffydd ap Llywelyn, expanding Edward's kingdom into this smaller country. During this conquest in 1063, Harold's brother, Tostig, fought by his side. One attacked the people of Wales by sea, while the other approached them by land. As a result, Gruffydd went into exile. Fear of what Harold might do caused the people to turn on the king of Wales, and after capturing Gruffydd, they beheaded him and presented the head to Harold to show that they supported him. This cemented his position as the under-king to Edward, who did not participate in the endeavor.

Tostig had supported his brother in the fight against Wales, but he proved to be a poor leader. Between his ruthless nature and the over-taxation of the people in his region, Northumbria, the people became dissatisfied with him. A revolt began in 1065, and Tostig could not put it down. Harold was forced to step in and restore order in the northern realm. To do this, though, he had to strip his brother of his title and send Tostig into exile, something that Tostig did not take well. There were rumors that Harold had managed to instigate the revolt in a bid to further gain Edward's trust and a place on the throne following the king's death. However, there was never any substantial evidence of this rumor.

In 1065, Harold married the widow of the King Gruffydd ap Llywelyn, Ealdgyth. Not only did this help provide a connection to Wales, but she was also related to earls in the northern part of the kingdom. This helped to extend Harold's power, which would have been the only real reason for the marriage. Harold had been romantically attached to Edith the Fair, also known as Edith Swanneck, and together, they had five children. It is said that Harold had married Edith Swanneck, but the marriage between Harold and Ealdgyth was the one that was deemed to be legitimate in the eyes of the clergy, and so, Edith Swanneck was seen as a mistress.

Claim to the Throne

Like King Harald of Norway, Harold Godwinson did not have any blood claim to the throne. However, his sister had been the wife of Edward the Confessor, which gave him about as much claim to the throne as William the Bastard. Since Harold had been working with the rightful king for so long, he actually made the most sense as the next king. He was also of Anglo-Saxon ancestry, while William was not.

The people of England had been ruled by the Romans hundreds of years before, and they had been under constant attack by the Vikings for the last couple hundred years. They wanted to keep the royal family Anglo-Saxon instead of having another ruler who did not understand their customs or traditions. With Harold having already established himself as a capable leader, they firmly supported him.

Events in Normandy

According to William the Bastard, Harold had pledged to support his claim to the throne during a visit to Normandy in 1064 CE. Edward the Confessor was said to have sent Harold to Normandy to talk with William, though what they were supposed to discuss has been subject to debate. Some speculate that it was for William to express Edward's desire that William become his heir, which is mainly based on what William later claimed was the case. Some say that Normandy was not even Harold's destination and that he and his men were blown off course on a trip to France and were subsequently captured by William and his men.

During his time in Normandy, Harold actually helped William by fighting for William against the Conan II, Duke of Brittany. For his help, William knighted Harold, at least according to the recordings that were added to the Bayeux Tapestry. However, it is also said that the only reason that William allowed Harold to leave was that he forced Harold Godwinson to promise that he would support William as the heir to the throne. This has been the account that has been passed down because William was the victor in the end, but that does not mean that the events actually occurred in the way that he claimed. For instance, the *Anglo-Saxon Chronicles* provide a completely different set of events of what happened in Normandy. According to their records, Harold's sole purpose in Normandy was to negotiate the release of English compatriots.

Either way, it is fairly clear that any oath that Harold took while in Normandy was done against his will and under duress. Both versions have reported that he was a captive of William's, though to different degrees. The fact that the oath was forced from him would have meant that it was not valid, and that is what the Anglo-Saxons believed.

History will never resolve exactly what happened during Harold's time in Normandy, though it is not entirely relevant. While they both had a better claim than King Harald of Norway, the best claim actually went to a living relative of King Æthelred II.

The Real Heir to the Throne

Edward may have died without any children, but his father had children from a previous marriage. They had been largely ignored because of how power-hungry Edward's mother, Emma of Normandy (King Æthelred II second wife), had been. She had been set on having her lineage on the throne, and she had ensured that by marrying Cnut after her first husband, King Æthelred II, died.

However, Edmund Ironside was King Æthelred II's eldest son, and it was his grandson, Edgar Ætheling, who had the best claim to the throne. Edmund's incredibly short reign saw England once again being ruled by a Viking usurper, pushing his rightful heir—his son named Edward the Exile, Edgar's father—out of the line of succession. King Æthelred II's second wife, Emma, would make sure that Edward the Exile would not rise to power, constantly putting her sons on the throne. However, as the second wife, her line should not have been the next on the throne. At the time of Edward the Confessor's death in 1066, Edgar was only a teenager. Many have speculated that Harold and other Anglo-Saxon nobles ensured that Edgar was kept from consideration, at least in part because of his age. Records of what happened were not kept, so it is only speculation as to what happened.

One strange thing to note was how quickly Harold's coronation had occurred following King Edward's death. It was not customary for a king to be crowned within a day of the death of the previous monarch. Given how rushed the coronation was, it appears that

Harold was trying to ensure that there was no time for any arguments or issues to arise because Edward had been childless when he died. With as dubious as the claims had been, they were only getting murkier. It was the perfect opportunity for Harold to finally establish his family as the rulers of the country. Unfortunately, for him, the hasty coronation did not stop others from seeking to claim the throne for themselves.

Following Harold's death at the Battle of Hastings, it does appear that the Anglo-Saxons finally suggested Edgar Ætheling be the next king. At only fifteen years old, he really would not have stood a chance against the much older and experienced William. Instead of trying to take his rightful place on the throne, he would eventually serve both William I and his son, William II. As William worked to stamp out the numerous rebellions, Edgar Ætheling spent time in Scotland from 1068 to 1072 with King Malcolm III Canmore. The Scottish king would face off against the fierce Norman army and would end up submitting. Edgar Ætheling again submitted to William's reign. By 1086, Edgar Ætheling was trusted enough by William I to lead the Norman forces, who were sent to the southern Italian city of Apulia in order to conquer it.

Edgar Ætheling would go on one of the early Crusades before England went through another civil war. During the next civil war, Edgar sided with the Duke of Normandy against the current English king, Henry I. They lost, and little is known of what happened to the man who should have been the king of England after 1106.

Chapter 6 – Verification of Events and Preparations for War

One thing that historians today agree on regarding the events prior to Edward's death was that something he said during William's visit to England in 1051 had been misunderstood by William as a promise that he would be the next king. This had made him think that he would eventually gain the crown of England without having to lift a finger.

Initially, even the Normans were not happy with the idea of invading England, and William was criticized for drawing them into yet another fight. It was only with the promise of new lands and titles that the Normans were convinced to back William the Bastard as the next King of England. This did not mean that the preparations went as smoothly as William could have wanted. Once he realized what was coming, Harold Godwinson had no less difficulty in trying to convince his people of the imminent danger that was coming from Normandy.

William's Reaction to Edward's Death

Word of King Edward's death reached William very quickly, interrupting a hunt that he and his men had been preparing to take on his lands. Since the coronation of Harold had happened so quickly, William learned both of Edward's death and Harold's coronation at the same time.

His reaction is easy to guess, and it was poetically described around one hundred years after the events of 1066. Anger gripped William as he honestly believed that Edward had actually promised it to him. It is almost certain that Edward had not meant anything when he made the promise, as he had dangled the crown in front of others before and after William, but William also likely believed that he was the best choice, so he was convinced that it had been a guarantee that he would be the heir to the English throne. There is also a very good chance that this is why he had never sought to expand into England before—he thought that all he had to do was survive Edward; after that, he was guaranteed the English crown.

Enraged that Harold would allow himself to be coronated, William realized that the position he thought would automatically become his was not so easily claimed. However, war was not his initial reaction. The two men had fought together on the same side, and William was not willing to attack without attempting to find a peaceful, less costly method first. This could be because of how different the two regions were and how they faced questions of power and expansion. Much of William's life had revolved around fighting and war. Many believe that he was illiterate and that he and his people were far less educated than the Anglo-Saxons were (in their eyes, they were potentially even more barbaric than Harald Hardrada and his Vikings). While revolts and problems had occurred during Edward's time, they were often resolved quickly, keeping the country from devolving into civil war. By comparison, the earldoms of France were constantly fighting and had little identity as a whole. They constantly sought to protect their lands and expand into that of their neighbors. This was in stark contrast to the English under Edward and Harold, who had developed an identity of the nations and were proud to be a part of it. The earls of Edward's kingdom rarely fought each other, with unrest usually occurring when one of the earls wronged the people on their lands. William and the other earls saw the peasants living on their land more as objects and cared little about what happened to them. Though he was religious, William often put himself over even the Church, making him less than ideal as the leader of the more peaceful island kingdom.

The other problem had to do with William's pride. For years, he had been telling people in Normandy and elsewhere in the French kingdom that he was the heir to the English throne. Now that the king was dead, Harold's coronation made a mockery of what William had been saying. The fact that he felt wronged both by Edward and Harold ensured that he would act, though, to his credit, William did attempt to find a peaceful resolution first.

Whatever his initial reaction was, William did not react with immediate wrath. Instead of storming off to attack the kingdom, he sent word to Harold, hoping to hear that it had been a mistake. Harold was adamant that he had been chosen by Edward and that he had already been made the king. There was just no going back now that the coronation had occurred. Of course, there are many questions about just how rapidly Harold had ensured that coronation. Even if he had been chosen to be king by Edward the Confessor and the people who had the final say (the Witan, also known as the Witenagemot, the Anglo-Saxon council which determined succession, resolved land grants, issued charters, managed church matters, and held considerable sway over the direction of the kingdom), the coronation was suspiciously fast, and no coronation had ever happened so quickly, especially with so many questions about who the rightful king was. Typically, those who felt they had a claim to the throne were given time to put forth their claim, but Harold had ensured that no one else was given that time. However, the death of King Edward around the religious holiday of Epiphany meant that all of the important people were already present. It is possible that the coronation was rushed because everyone was already there, and putting it off would have made them either have to remain or return soon after the holiday. In the end, it could have been an issue of convenience over any rush on Harold's part. Since what has come down was from the Norman perspective, the real reason for the rapidity of Harold's coronation could have been obscured by the conquerors to give William's claim more legitimacy and to erode Harold's claim.

Some historians say that William had made a second effort to peacefully resolve the dispute by asking if Harold would marry his daughter. This is dubious, for if William had tried to ensure that Harold would fulfill a promise to marry his daughter, it would be out of character for the Norman earl. Once he felt insulted, especially how publicly he had been humiliated when word arrived of Edward's death, William often prepared for war. He had already given Harold a chance for peace; offering a second option does not seem likely. However, if this did occur, broken betrothals were entirely common at the time. Considering the age difference between Harold (44 years old) and William's daughter Agatha (about 8 years old), it would have meant that Harold would have had to wait until she reached puberty to marry her. He also already had Edith Swanneck (who the church considered to be a mistress), whose relationship is perhaps comparable to a common-law wife today. And not long after his coronation, he married Ealdgyth of Mercia. So, marriage to William's daughter was not really an option.

Harold did have the opportunity, though, to apologize more sincerely or to try to come up with a compromise. He had built much of his reputation on his ability to come to peaceful terms with his adversaries when it was possible. For a man with this kind of reputation, this was perhaps his greatest failing when it came to the issue of succession. However, Harold also had to abide by what the Witan said, and they did not have a reason to apologize for his coronation. As far as they were concerned, William did not have a claim to the throne, and they felt no need to try to pacify him. With this final denial of any claim William or his family may have had, William decided there was only one way to resolve the damage that had been done to his pride.

Within a month of his coronation, King Harold realized how much of a mistake it had been to be as unmoving as he had been when dealing with William. Whatever their relationship was before January of 1066, they were now enemies. And William was a very dangerous enemy to have.

A Hard Sell and War Preparations

Both rulers had their own problems with trying to convince people about the necessity of the war. For William, the problem was in selling the idea of going to war, especially after he had already told everyone that he was the English heir. Fighting to take lands so far from home had never been something that the Normans had considered, and there was no obvious reason for them to invade England. There was more than enough political intrigue and fighting at home to keep them occupied without risking to go so far away to unfamiliar lands. Initially, it seemed more like a vanity war that William was dragging them into.

Meanwhile, King Harold spent months trying to make his people understand the grave danger they were in as he had already seen what William could do. The southern parts of the kingdom were not accustomed to preparing for danger, as they often waited until the last minute when the danger was visible to them. Much of the kingdom operated that way because, apart from the Viking raids, they had lived more peacefully than the people of the continental kingdoms.

To rally people to his cause, William held up the relationship he had with Edward, which had been positive. Because of the promise William felt Edward had made to him, he worked to convince the people that the throne had been stolen from him. The reluctance of the nobles was relatively quickly broken down as William promised them that the English lands would be divided among them, proving that William had little intention of upholding the power structure in England. Given the fact that the English nobles and the Witan had given Harold the crown, there was likely some resentment. Once

William procured the consent of the pope to attack, he was able to put his plan of attack in action.

By the summer of 1066, the English were more than willing to listen to Edward's warnings, and he had amassed a much larger force to face the danger he knew was coming from Normandy. According to the *Anglo-Saxon Chronicle*, it was the largest force that had ever been gathered in the kingdom. The army was made up of nobles and their housecarls (similar to a knight). According to the Vikings, who had encountered the fierce housecarls, they were as capable as two soldiers. Unfortunately, there were not many housecarls, and the kingdom did not have a standing army, as armies were too expensive (and largely unnecessary in England). Much of the army was composed of citizens who were required by law to serve in the military for two months a year. There were also some peasants who could be ordered to serve in the military by the earl or the person in charge of a particular region.

Harold also managed to build an unprecedented naval force that included ships that followed the designs commonly used by the Vikings to carry cargo. They were not as effective as the Viking longships that were used in raids, but when the ships were originally commissioned, which was before Harold had become king, warfare had not been the primary concern.

The problem was that the first battle did not come from William. It was King Harald and Harold's brother Tostig who would prove to be the first to strike in a bid to take the throne.

Chapter 7 – The Invasion of the Norwegian King Harald Hardrada

Though he had the least claim to the English throne, King Harald Hardrada was undeterred. There had never been a point in his life where he would simply give up without trying. Though he had not been as successful at uniting the continental kingdom that Cnut had managed, Harald felt that he could take on the English with more success. The idea that he could succeed was bolstered by the fact that he was able to get someone on his side who knew King Harold II well—his brother Tostig.

Eyeing the Isle and Forming Alliances

Just as Norway's political climate had drastically changed during Harald's time away, England had changed significantly after King Cnut's death. His sons, Harold Harefoot and then Harthacnut, had not ruled for too long, a combined seven years between them. After their reigns, England was back under the control of the Anglo-Saxons, first going to Edward the Confessor and then Harold Godwinson. No longer under the control of any Viking king, the Anglo-Saxons had become accustomed to being under the control of one of their own, and they were far less likely to welcome any foreign invaders.

Like he had done when trying to take Denmark from Magnus I, Harald looked for people close to King Harold with whom he could ally. And in doing so, he found Tostig Godwinson. Unlike his brother Harold, Tostig was not on good terms with King Edward the Confessor, resulting in his removal from his Northumbrian earldom. Tostig felt that his brother had betrayed him as it was Harold who ultimately had him pushed out as the earl of Northumbria. He had been a harsh leader during his time as earl, and Harold really did not have much choice but to remove him to end the Northumbrian civil war that had resulted from discontentment under Tostig's rule. King Edward may have been willing to allow Tostig to continue, but Harold had greater control over the secular rule of the lands, much as his father had before him. It is not certain why Harold was so willing to turn on his brother, but it is likely that the pressure and power of the rebels helped to persuade him that his brother could not manage the region peacefully. While Tostig had helped to bring some stability to the region, his methods had caused the revolt. Feeling betrayed, Tostig went to Flanders and then sought to provide assistance to attack England when the opportunity arose. In a strange twist of fate, he had initially offered his services to William of Normandy. However, William did not feel that he needed Tostig's help as Tostig's plans often were not well thought out, and he also seemed a bit unstable.

Knowing that he would need more help than Tostig could provide, Harald also allied with the chieftains in Shetland and Orkney. They were Scottish, but the lands were under the control of Norway. Feeling that he had enough men to be victorious, Harald finally made his move and began the invasion of England.

The Battle of Fulford (September 20th, 1066)

With 10,000 men, Harald landed in northern England at the mouth of the River Tees. Initially, he attacked using the traditional lightning strikes of his people, tormenting the English people who lived along the coast. Harald and his forces worked their way south to Scarborough, where they burned the town down because the townspeople put up fierce resistance to the invaders. Following this brutal display, the people of the Northumbrian region were far less willing to fight back against the invaders.

The destruction that King Harald of Norway was bringing along the coast soon became impossible for King Harold II of England to ignore, so he deployed forces north to face the invaders. Sending 5,000 men, the Anglo-Saxon king faced off against the battle-hardened Vikings at Fulford. Harald's men had the advantage, both because his forces were twice the size of the English king's and because the terrain was marshy, which was easier for Harald's people to navigate.

For the first time since they had invaded England, Harald and his men achieved a decisive victory against the Anglo-Saxons.

The Tide Turns at the Battle of Stamford Bridge (September 25th, 1066)

King Harold II had only been king of England for almost ten months by this point. Desperate to keep the country under his control, he marched to the front of his forces and pushed them to move more than 190 miles north to where the Viking invaders had stationed themselves.

King Harold and King Harald met again at the Battle of Stamford Bridge.

Much of this story was told by Snorri Sturluson, the author of *King Harald's Saga*, so some of the events should be taken with a grain of salt. What is certain is that Harald had not expected the English to march north to engage his troops, giving Harold II the element of surprise. It is likely that what the Viking king was expecting was an exchange of hostages, as was typically agreed to after a major battle. Instead, he found an English army now marching toward him and his army, and the English army was much larger than it had been at Fulford. It is estimated that King Harold II had amassed a force of around 13,000 men. In comparison, the Vikings had between 7,000 to 9,000 men, although some of these men joined later in the battle. This was because the Vikings were resting, meaning they were not equipped to fight, with most of them not even wearing their heavy armor, and the Viking forces were spread across two sides of the local river, the River Derwent.

The Viking forces that were on the wrong side of the river tried to cross the bridge to their armory so that they could fight together as a unit, but the English charged them, killing many before the Vikings could return to the main part of the camp.

An interesting legend from this time (recorded in the *Anglo-Saxon Chronicle*) relayed a story of a single Viking standing on the bridge to create a choke point against the English. He was able to kill forty Anglo-Saxons before one of them snuck under the bridge and killed him with a spear.

By the time the English forces crossed the bridge, the Vikings had had enough time to regroup and form a shield wall against them. The chaos that ensued must have irked Harald. Going into a berserker rage, he threw himself into the advancing English army. It is said that during his rage, the king was struck in the neck by an arrow, and he perished on the field. Without their king, the Vikings no longer had the drive to continue to face the Anglo-Saxon forces. Harold's brother Tostig was also killed during this battle, giving the Vikings no claim to the throne.

King Harald is sometimes referred to as the last of the great Vikings. He did not back down and continued many of the tactics for which his people had become famous. Sometimes he divided his people, while at other times he sought to unite them, always under his own banner. Unwavering in his courage and sometimes obstinate to a fault, he was the last Viking king who embodied the virtues and ideals of the Vikings as we know them today.

Chapter 8 – William Arrives in England

The last time England was successfully invaded was 1066, a year that had already seen so much turmoil and uncertainty. The events leading up to William's arrival in England actually played into his favor. King Harold II and his men had recently fought with King Harald in the north. Whether or not he knew about King Harald's attack, William's timing could not have been better, for it was on September 28th, 1066, that he landed in southern England at Pevensey Bay.

Significant Events and Battles of 1066

(*Source: https://en.wikipedia.org/wiki/File:Norman-conquest-1066.svg*)

William's First Actions

The omens were good for William and his planned conquest. After having waited for nearly two months to make the crossing based on the right winds, those winds and favorable conditions finally began one day after the Battle of Stamford Bridge. This meant that Harold II was far to the north, although it is unlikely that William knew that as he and his men left the continent the next day. One day later, they made landfall on the island. The Battle of Samford Bridge was on September 25th, 1066; the Norman invasion began on September 28th, 1066. The timing could not have been more perfect for William, and little could have made the timing worse for Harold II. With this situation, the Normans could have easily believed that this was a sign that William was the rightful king, adding further religious righteousness to their cause.

Upon his arrival in England, William began to raid the towns and villages in the area. This was effective, not only because it brought terror to the Anglo-Saxons, but it was also the area that Harold's family came from. William had been aboard the ship *Mora* when they landed, the largest and fastest of the 700 or more ships used during the invasion, and it is likely that he did not know too much about the coastline, as they had only planned the invasion for a few months. Until January 1066, he had never had any reason to survey the lands or to consider an invasion. However, he likely would have known of its importance to Harold II. Some historians speculate that the reason they landed in Pevensey was because of the tides. They would not want to sail out of the area against the tides, so they docked and began their invasion, attacking those in the surrounding area.

At the time, Pevensey was primarily a market town, not a village. With the summer over, there were fewer soldiers around to protect the people in the area as they had gone home after the end of summer. When William and the Normans invaded, the people in England could see them coming, but they did not have any protection against them. Since most of them were merchants, farmers, and ranchers, their only real course of action was to try to hide from the invaders.

In the Bayeux Tapestry, the men are shown without their helmets at this time. This would indicate that they did not expect much resistance in the beginning. William would likely have known about the different towns, villages, and populations in the area and what they were likely to encounter. The tapestry would later depict the Normans as having helmets when they fought at the Battle of Hastings, so it was very likely that the Normans knew they were primarily going to be conducting raids instead of actually fighting when they arrived. This would have given them the base they needed for their men. Considering they arrived in a market town, they were able to better supply the troops with food and potable water, as they had not been well provisioned prior to leaving the continent.

Knowing that they had at least a few days before Harold II and his army could arrive (not knowing that they would actually have a couple of weeks), they were able to build a small round fort just inside one of the Roman walls built several centuries earlier. The fort was constructed of wood, and they dug a trench around it within a matter of a couple of days. This provided them with a place where they could plan their next moves.

Initially, William set out with William FitzOsbern, who was a distant cousin, and several of his knights to scout the area after the construction of the fort. They departed on horseback, but their lack of familiarity with the land soon proved to be a source of embarrassment. The men returned from their reconnaissance mission by foot because of how difficult it was for the horses on the terrain. The lands of Normandy were nothing like the lands of southern England, a factor that the Normans had not considered. The lands were wetter, with a lot of marshland in the area, making it much harder to traverse.

Though they had already created a fort, the Normans decided to leave the area. The embarrassing scouting incident, which was certainly undignified for the short-tempered Norman leader, was not the only reason to leave Pevensey, though. Only one reliable road went in and out of the area, and it had been built while the Romans had been in control of the area. This road did eventually lead to London, but there was no other direction for them to go if needed.

When they left, the Normans were quick to start striking fear in the hearts of the people. Some of the villages in the area were left alone, but many were not so lucky. One of the ways that historians have determined where the Normans raided was through the value placed on villages and towns in the area according to the Domesday Book, which was commissioned over a decade later (more information about this book is located in chapter 11). The book reflects the value of the population areas and the region, and some of the villages were marked as *wasta*, indicating that they had been laid to waste during the invasion. The trail of Norman destruction would go from Pevensey all the way to Hastings, which was where they would finally face their enemy and change the entire trajectory of the future of England.

Some historians have postulated that William encouraged his men to conduct raids as a way of drawing Harold down to the area. However, it is more likely that they conducted warfare in England the same they had anywhere else. Fighting on the continent had included raiding and pillaging every place that they went, so it would have taken a major intervention to stop the men from doing what they likely saw as natural. The fighters on the continent saw the slaughtering and destruction of civilians and towns as a part of warfare, not as a crime as it is viewed today. This is why it is somewhat ironic that William had promised lands to the Normans since population centers were destroyed upon their arrival. Then again, it is likely that the people who had been promised lands would have known that rebuilding would be necessary, making it a calculated risk that they were willing to make.

The Normans again constructed a fort that they could use in Hastings. From it, the Normans raided all of the surrounding areas. Only two towns were not destroyed during this time: Hastings and Westfield. Hastings was spared because they had made it their hub. However, historians are not sure why Westfield was spared the same treatment as the other villages in the area.

Harold's Mistake – Disbanding the Army at the End of Summer

Nearly as soon as they had finished eliminating the threat of King Harald and Tostig, Harold II and his men received word that the Normans had invaded in the south. Having spent time with William of Normandy a few years previously, and then engaging in their tense exchange following Harold II's coronation, the king likely knew that the Norman invasion was a serious threat to his crown, as well as his people. Harold would have known that he could not waste time.

The timing of the invasion was terrible for King Harold II for two reasons, firstly because of how it dovetailed with a northern invasion. The other was that Harold had been waiting in the southern part of the country for most of the summer because he knew that William's arrival was imminent. The question was when he would invade, not if he would. Harold had men stationed both on land and at sea for most of the summer in preparation for the inevitable. At the time, standing armies really did not exist. The men who were stationed in the south had to return home for the harvest, so on September 8th, Harold disbanded the militia.

It was only a few weeks later that Harald Hardrada invaded, causing Harold to rush north with what men he had. Despite their decisive victory, the Anglo-Saxons had suffered great losses of the men who were available to fight. The king's only real option was to rally men to the Anglo-Saxon cause as they marched south as quickly as possible.

Many of the earls in the northern parts of the country chose not to assist with the southern invasion as they did not feel that they were directly threatened by the invaders. Still, the king did enlist people from the areas that they passed through on their way to confront the invaders. As soon as he and his current force reached London, the king sent word out to other earls that he needed additional support to stop the latest invasion. Perhaps as word of the chaos and destruction that the Normans had been wrecking on his former Wessex earldom reached him, Harold II became anxious to move out and stop him. The knights and men of the higher social class rode south on horses, while anyone else who joined them traveled on foot. Harold II had lost a large number of his housecarls in the northern battle, meaning that he was in a much weaker position when he marched south than he had been when he first headed north to confront Harald Hardrada.

Some of his supporters would criticize the king for his hasty decision to attack soon after they arrived near Hastings. There were still men who were responding to the call when Harold II decided to engage the Normans. It is perhaps this decision that would lead to the events of that October day, but it is also possible that waiting for more support would not have changed the events. What is known is that King Harold II would not delay his attack when he was within striking distance of his latest enemy.

Chapter 9 – The Battle of Hastings and William's Coronation

At the beginning of September 1066, there was nothing particularly interesting about Hastings, nothing that would have even hinted at the pivotal event that would occur about a month and a half later. When William and the Normans set up in the area, they all but destroyed the area, so they would not have been able to remain there over the course of the winter.

Fortunately for the Normans, though, Harold II and his men arrived before the winter began. The battle actually occurred about six and a half miles away, in the small town known as Battle today. It was located northwest of Hastings, but as one of the few places that still remained in the region, the battle was named after the place where William and his men had stationed themselves.

Today, we are accustomed to wars dragging out for years, with our leaders sitting far from the fighting. During the Middle Ages, however, the leaders fought their own battles since soldiers would often not follow a man who was not willing to put his life on the line to show his dedication to his claims. This meant that if the leader of one of the armies died, the end of a battle could be a decisive victory for the other side. However, as William would find out, winning a battle and killing King Harold II was not the end of the war.

Still, the Battle of Hastings did successfully answer the question of who would reign as king. A year that had begun with the death of King Edward the Confessor would end with the coronation of King William I. Had Harold II been victorious at Hastings, the history of the island nation would have been very different from what we know today.

On the Eve of Battle

Harold II and his men had marched about 200 miles within a week to reach Hastings, which was an impressive feat back then. This was an average of thirty miles every day, which started about a week after Harold stopped in London. By October 13th, both of the armies were in southern England, about eight miles apart from each other, which shows just how quickly Harold II had marched his men down to stop William.

Given that the battle happened about 950 years ago, there is a lot that we do not know, such as how many men followed William and Harold II into battle. The numbers given for both varies because it is unlikely that either side actually took the time to count their forces before the battle started. According to modern estimates, it is thought that Harold II had between 7,000 to 12,000 men, while William had between 5,000 and 13,000 men.

Based on the scenes depicted on the Bayeux Tapestry, both men had established similar forces, including cavalry and archers. However, Harold II had fewer archers than his enemy, which gave William a distinct advantage, besides his men being more well-rested. Some speculate that Harold II would have had a greater contingent of archers if he had taken a more measured approach. Archers would almost certainly have moved on foot, which meant that many of them were likely still making their way south. It is almost certain that Harold II had pressed south as quickly as possible to protect the earldom that had been in his family for so long. Had he been less hasty, his men may have been better matched against the effective Norman archers who used crossbows.

Final Preparations

When the morning of October 14th began, the two leaders were setting up their men in formations that they felt would play best against the strategies and forces of the other. Harold II and his higher-ranking men had traveled on horse, but the English did not typically use horses in battle. William and the Normans did. This meant that the Normans would be sending their cavalry in to fight against a thick wall of Anglo-Saxon soldiers on foot.

The Anglo-Saxon forces were established in a long line that is estimated to have been about half a mile long. They were stationed on a hill, giving them the upper ground. Their men had shields, meaning that their defense was more like a shield wall, which would have been incredibly difficult for the Norman cavalry to penetrate. To thwart the cavalry, the Anglo-Saxons had chosen to sacrifice maneuverability because the men were lined up almost shoulder to shoulder.

William had several different peoples to manage, which included the Normans, Bretons, and French forces. He stationed them based on their origins, with the Normans acting as the core of his forces. The other two groups were placed on the west and east. In addition to dividing his forces based on where they had learned to fight, the soldiers were put in formation based on their role in the fight. Archers were placed in the front to take down as many of the Anglo-Saxon men in the shield wall as possible. The next part of their forces was the infantry, followed by the knights who were to ride in on their horses. Once the archers had weakened the wall, the infantry would scatter them, and then the cavalry would kill the men who remained.

This showed two very different approaches to fighting. William and his men valued mobility and the flexibility to move across the lands. In contrast, Harold II and his men were more like the woods behind them. Their success required them to hold strong and to resist breaking against the highly mobile Normans. This is likely what caused the battle to continue longer than other battles of the era. Neither side had fought a battle against an enemy with such a different approach to their own. The Anglo-Saxon approach was more like the Roman fighting style, where soldiers stood in tight formation, while the Normans used a style that was more like what we

associate with the Middle Ages.

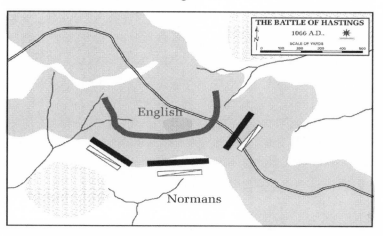

English and Norman Formations

(*Source:*
https://upload.wikimedia.org/wikipedia/commons/9/91/Battle_of_Ha stings%2C_1066.png)

The Fighting Starts – One of the Longest Battles at That Time

During the 11th century, battles usually only lasted a couple of hours. With all of the heavy gear and with so many men, fighting for long periods of time was generally detrimental. The Battle of Hastings would not follow the typical battle duration, though, as it lasted for nearly the entire day.

According to the Norman version of events, William surprised Harold and his men. This is probably an exaggerated or entirely inaccurate account, as Harold and his men were in position for the battle. It would not be out of place for propaganda to occur in order to try to give the victorious William greater glory and more credit than was actually earned.

According to another account, both sides sounded the trumpets, initiating the battle at 9 a.m. The grounds before them would have been fairly easy to maneuver, something that was not true of some of the surrounding areas. As William had found out in Pevensey, not all of the terrain was suited for cavalry or fighting. Not only would this have been a reason to settle in Hastings to wait for Harold II to attack, but it also gave his man better grounds to fight. However, the strategy of the English was to give themselves an area where they could more quickly retreat if needed. Behind the English were woods, though their formation was meant to be the protection they needed in the battle. If they needed to flee, the woods might have provided them with a better means of escape since it would have been more difficult for the cavalry to chase them in the bramble.

When the trumpets sounded, the Norman archers began to shoot a volley of their arrows against the wall of Anglo-Saxon warriors. The Anglo-Saxons responded nearly immediately as the Norman archers stepped out of the way. While they did not have many archers, they were armed with javelins and other weapons they could throw. It appears that some of the other projectiles that they launched against the invaders were sticks that had stones attached to them and, more interestingly, axes. William's plan to scatter Harold's men after the initial volley was quickly proven to be less effective than he had expected. Harold's men not only repelled the Norman foot soldiers but their cavalry as well.

Considering the first noted action of the battle was done by the archers, it is expected that the first fatalities were likely on the Anglo-Saxon side. Given that the records today come from the conquering side, the first death that was recorded belonged to the Normans. According to some accounts, the first person to die (at least on the Norman side) was someone close to the king—his jester named Taillefer.

This unexpected result caused panic among William's men. As some of them turned to retreat from a wall of soldiers that had not broken as expected, those behind them thought that the battle was turning against them. Some even thought that perhaps William had been killed during the initial skirmish. Parts of the wall broke as some of the Anglo-Saxons chased the fleeing men. When William went charging into the fray, his forces realized that he had not been killed. Soon, the men who had broken from the shield wall were eliminated as the invaders took heart in William's charge against the enemy.

There is a lot of speculation about what the Anglo-Saxons could have done differently that would have changed the events of what happened next. If the shield wall had pushed forward instead of breaking to pursue the Normans, they might have been successful. It is also said that they could have moved back together, holding the line that had already proven to be nearly impenetrable to William and his men. However, the Anglo-Saxons allowed themselves to be partially divided after having withstood the initial onslaught.

Despite this mistake, the wall did reform, and it remained strong over the course of the day, a feat that was likely physically punishing as they were limited in their movements. The Norman reports of the events showed their awe at how well-trained the English were against their advances.

After hours of fighting, William decided to use what he had learned from the first hours of the battle against the Anglo-Saxons. Ordering his cavalry to leave the field, he drew out more of the men who had been standing strong against them. After a greater portion of the shield wall had been broken, William ordered his men to turn and annihilate those who had broken away.

This second wave occurred after a long day of fighting. After this second wave of attacks proved to be successful against them, the English saw no way out but to surrender.

The only thing that is certain is that Harold II died that day. What happened to him has been a source of debate, with some saying that he was killed by an arrow to the eye or the neck. Others say he was cut down on the battlefield. The loyal soldiers of his royal guard did continue to fight without him for a while, as they did not see the invader as being a legitimate king. They gathered around the body of Harold II and fought until the very end. There was a defensive action carried out by the Anglo-Saxons at a site known as the "Malfosse," but it is unknown what happened there, except for the fact that they seriously wounded Eustace II of Boulogne before being defeated.

After fighting for most of the day, and with their king dead, the shield wall had finally dissolved. The Anglo-Saxons broke and tried to flee. A large portion of those who fled reached a rampart that would provide them with some protection against the Normans who were pursuing them. With the light waning, the Normans found themselves in trouble as they could not really see, and the grounds were not familiar to them. Struggling through the long grass in the growing darkness, many of them ended up struggling and falling through the less sturdy, marshy grounds. It became too difficult for them to progress, which gave the surviving Anglo-Saxons one final advantage, as the English were able to make short work of many of the men who had tried to pursue them.

Unfortunately for the English, it was not enough. They had lost their king and many of the nobility who had followed him south.

The battle had lasted an unimaginable nine hours, with both sides exhausted by the time the fighting ceased. The Norman's mobility had allowed them to try some deceptive tactics to lure the Anglo-Saxons to break their ranks, which had some mild success. However, that would have taken a real toll on them as they would have had to repeatedly go up the hill where the English had formed their line. William himself was said to have lost three horses during the repeated charges. It is unknown when King Harold II had been killed, though some say that it was likely during the last Norman charge. With the English continuing to fight even after his death, the Normans could not have been sure of their victory until the very end of the battle. It was clear that the two sides were evenly matched, and any small changes in their forces or strategies could have completely changed the end results.

Harold II Laid to Rest

Just like King Harold II's death was obscured by different stories of his demise, the events surrounding the fate of his remains are not fully known. According to some stories, his mother had offered to pay a large sum of gold for his body so that he could be properly buried. However, William refused to return the body.

According to another story, Harold's long-time partner, Edith Swanneck, had gone to the site of the battle to identify him. He had been so badly mutilated that it was nearly impossible to identify him, so only his lover could say for certain that the corpse was his. If this story is true, then it would have been almost certain that he had not been killed by an arrow but by repeated attacks by the Normans on the battlefield.

In a third version, the one that was most widely repeated in the 12th century, said that he was finally laid to rest in Waltham Holy Cross located in Essex. This would later prove to be untrue as the tomb was opened to reveal that his remains were not there.

There is even a version of events that indicate just how difficult it was for him to accept defeat; according to this version, Harold had not been killed but had gone on to live elsewhere as a hermit until he was old. This is absolutely untrue, but it would have likely been something that William would have encouraged others to believe.

In all likelihood, the first story is the most likely scenario. By denying the Anglo-Saxons their king's body, William denied them a spiritual place around which they could rally. Stories were able to spring up around what had happened, some which even cast doubt on the fact that Harold II died during this battle. This denied the king his status as a martyr for the cause of the Anglo-Saxons. Whatever happened to Harold's body is lost to time due to the rumors and speculation about its fate.

Chapter 10 – Rebelling against the New King and the Consequences of Doing So

Harold II may have been killed during the Battle of Hastings, but the Anglo-Saxons were not willing to simply accept William of Normandy as their king. He had never lived in the country, did not have a legitimate claim in their eyes, and he had killed the king the Witan had elected. This led to a lot of resistance against William and his nobles.

A March across the South

Harold II and two of his brothers were killed during the Battle of Hastings, removing some of the best protectors of the Wessex earldom. Without their protectors, the more pastoral areas of southern England offered little challenge against the Normans. Places like Dover, Canterbury, and Winchester quickly fell to William and his forces. Then he turned his attention to the only place that could really hope to withstand his march across the region— London. Without their king to rally them, the people of London could not put up the kind of fight that was required to keep William from finally conquering the capital. By Christmas Day, William the

Bastard was crowned William I. However, taking over the southern portions of the kingdom did not mean that the rest of the realms would accept him. And the other earls were not the only problem William would face. Edgar Ætheling was chosen by some to rule, but he was still just a teenager at the time. His ability to win would have been small, and he did not seem eager to press his claim to the throne.

It is interesting to consider how little he was actually prepared for what would happen after he became king of England. For a man who blindly believed a vague promise that he would be the next king, William I did precious little to understand the realm that he was going to rule. He did not have much of an understanding of the power structures in the country, nor did he understand his enemies. All of the problems that Edward the Confessor and Harold II had faced in ruling the lower kingdom on the island (Scotland was an entirely different nation at this time) would become unexpected issues for the new ruler.

Perhaps one of the best omens of how much difficulty he would encounter happened on the day that should have been celebratory: the day of William I's coronation.

A New King

Though William would continue to fight, the Battle of Hastings all but ensured he would be made king, no matter how the Anglo-Saxons felt about him. And on Christmas Day 1066, he was crowned king.

There are two primary records, the Bayeux Tapestry and the *Anglo-Saxon Chronicle*, that we can use to get a better glimpse at the chaos that occurred during 1066. However, neither of them provides details about the coronation. It is believed that the tapestry once included William I's coronation, but the end of the tapestry has been lost. The *Anglo-Saxon Chronicle* manuscripts are largely silent on this period. It is likely that they were upset by the loss of so many of their nobles and the success of an invader who had never shown an interest in their lands until Edward the Confessor had died.

William of Poitiers would write about the coronation and other events several years after William's victory. From this account, we have more details of the coronation, though there are definitely aspects that should be taken with several large grains of salt. According to him, "all shouted their joyful assent, with no hesitation, as if heaven had granted them one mind and one voice." In this, he also says that the English were celebrating their new king and were happy to be his subjects. Considering the little that was said about it in the *Anglo-Saxon Chronicle*, it is almost certain that this is little more than propaganda. While the Normans who were to get lands out of the conquest would have cheered for William, there was no reason for the English to welcome him. The new king was soon to give their lands away to foreigners who had backed him. He was just another invader usurping their throne under a claim that they did not believe. Perhaps the only reason why they would agree to William being king was in the hopes that they could minimize their losses under this new, more barbaric king.

William of Poitiers may have portrayed the cries as those of "joyful assent," but the series of events that followed it is a much more likely indicator of the proper interpretation of any cries from outside of the abbey where the new king was crowned. Guards in the abbey quickly exited to see what was happening, and once outside, they thought that the cries were a sign of treachery. In response, they began to set fire to the homes in the immediate area, lighting the city on fire. People began trying to fight the flames, losing interest in the coronation because of the fear of losing everything they owned.

This turned out to be an apt beginning to William I's reign. The lands around him burned, yet he continued with his plans forward. The first five years would prove to be the most difficult, largely because of his ignorance of the people and their problems. In response to the Anglo-Saxon's rejection of him, William and his men would plunder the country, claiming the wealth that the English had accumulated over the years. Even if they had accepted him, William had made promises to the Normans and others on the continent to get them to back his invasion. Plundering the wealth of the island was nearly a certainty because he had to make good on these promises. This would have given the native peoples a reason to keep rejecting him until he finally and brutally put down their attempts to overthrow them.

That Christmas Day in 1066 was an ominous sign of just what was to come.

Constant Troubles from the Natives, Long-standing Enemies, and an Unlikely Alliance

The Anglo-Saxons were not eager to welcome an invader, and this was quickly shown in repeated attacks against the Normans. The remaining members of the Godwin family, particularly Harold II's children, caused issues for William I. His sons instigated two of their own invasions after taking refuge in Ireland, where their father had spent his year of exile under Edward the Confessor. The earls of the northern realms were no less accepting, and a rebellion against William began in York. The new king was able to stop both of the Godwin invasions and the rebellion. The York rebellion proved to be more difficult, though, so William I ended up employing the barbaric tactics that were frequently used on the continent to put down the rebellion. Over the winter of 1069 and into the beginning of 1070, he took a scorched-earth approach to terrifying and crippling those who denied his claim. Like he had done in the south during the initial invasion, William burned villages to the ground, destroyed crops, and slaughtered the livestock.

Over time, nearly all of the old Anglo-Saxon families who had ruled over the different regions were removed in favor of Normans. To ensure that they were protected, William the Conqueror had castles constructed all around his kingdom. This was meant to provide places where his faithful followers would be safe, as soldiers could be stationed across the lands that were rejecting his rule.

William's victory near Hastings did not quell the problems of the countries that were frequent antagonists to the Anglo-Saxon people. While William I was fighting against Harold's children and against the York rebellion, he also faced attacks from Wales. Harold II had managed to subdue them, but they saw an opportunity to strike back against the new English king. William successfully repelled those attacks, but he did not take control of the country.

The people of Wales were not the only ones who saw the conquest as an opportunity. The Vikings had been a constant thorn in the side of Britain, and following William's coronation, they again started to raid the coast, as they had been doing on and off for centuries. Over the centuries, the Vikings had developed a strategy of raiding England whenever there were signs of problems in the country. Obviously, the changing of hands of the throne was not an opportunity that they could ignore. From their perspective, it was the perfect time to test out the new king who clearly did not know the history behind their attacks and so would likely not know how best to counter them.

The Vikings soon found an unlikely ally in the people who had once been staunchly opposed to them—the Anglo-Saxon nobles. An alliance was formed in September 1069 between King Sweyn II of Denmark and the English rebels who wanted the kingdom restored to their people. The Danish king sent 300 ships to York, led by his brother Asbjørn, where they were welcomed by the half-great-nephew of Edward the Confessor, Edgar Ætheling, who had begun a rebellion in York earlier that year but managed to escape unscathed. Together, the Vikings and the Anglo-Saxon rebels captured many of the commanders, who were then ransomed off to fund the fighting. Most of the troops who were not ransomed, whether because their family could not pay or because the troops were of common birth, were killed outright.

When William received word of this, he marched an army to York, only to find that the Vikings had already departed. The Danes had fled along the River Trent with a substantial amount of wealth that they had taken from the city and surrounding area. As he did not have a fleet, William could not pursue the Danes. The only recourse he had was the traditional Anglo-Saxon method of repulsing the Vikings—he had to pay them to leave (since generally all the Vikings sought was wealth from their raids). Asbjørn took the money, but he did not hold up his end of the bargain. Instead, he and his men hunkered down for the winter in the marshes around Lincolnshire. By avoiding any direct contact against William's forces, the Danish did not suffer the same fate as the Anglo-Saxons did around York.

However, they were affected by William's scorched-earth policy. By the time winter ended in early 1070, the Vikings who had remained were starving and weakened after the cold winter. Their spirits were soon lifted as King Sweyn II arrived with reinforcements. An initial assessment of the remaining forces likely caused him to abandon any idea of a full-scale invasion, though. Instead, he opted to conduct the typical raids. During this time, he encountered Hereward the Wake, an Anglo-Saxon who had lost everything to the Normans and now lived on a small island called Ely. Hereward's exploits were recorded, and they captured the imagination of people over the next couple of centuries. Over time, his life would become a tale of a man seeking to reclaim the lands that were taken from him. This shows that even long after the Norman established themselves, some resentment lingered after the king had died.

Together, the King Sweyn II and Hereward the Wake began a march against Peterborough. The *Anglo-Saxon Chronicle* claims that they targeted Peterborough because William I was going to appoint a new abbot there. During May and June of 1070, they sacked the abbey, where the Norman Turold of Fécamp was to become abbot. According to some sources, the sacking of this religious place was justified because they did not want the wealth to be taken by the

Normans. This was actually a legitimate fear, as William I had been raiding other monasteries and religious facilities to pay his army. It is also possible that Hereward had wanted to use the money from the abbey to pay for his own army.

However, it was the Vikings who decided what would happen with the riches they had stolen. Claiming most of it for themselves, they decided that they did not need to remain any longer in England. After extorting more money out of William I to leave, the Danish Vikings tried to return home in 1070 CE. After breaking the alliance with Hereward and absconding with most of the wealth, the Vikings found that karma was not too far behind them. Most of the ships and the majority of the booty they had taken over the year were sunk as they made their way back to the continent.

The loss of his Viking allies did not seem to deter Hereward from his goal, which is likely why he gained such a prominent place in the stories passed down after his death. Determined to be a thorn in William's side, he would successfully establish a base for his rebels at Ely Abbey. The subsequent guerrilla campaigns against the Normans attracted the attention of other Anglo-Saxon rebels. When 1071 began, the small contingent of Anglo-Saxon rebels that were left after the Vikings deserted them had grown to a much larger threat, which included three other notable leaders: Æthelwine (once the bishop of Durham), Morcar (once the earl of Northumbria), and Waltheof (a powerful noble of Northumbria).

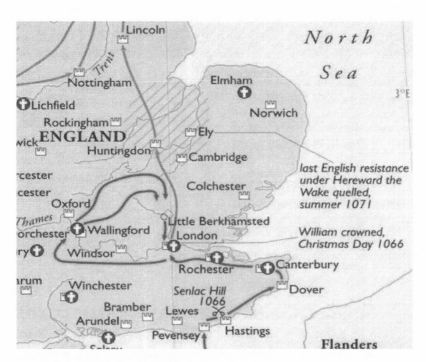

Last Major Anglo-Saxon Resistance

(Source: https://www.ancient.eu/image/9866/a-map-indicating-the-ely-rebellion-of-the-norman-c/)

William had sent a few expeditions against them, but it became clear that they were not going to be able to quickly stifle the growing rebellion as they had during the winter of 1069, and so, William marched north to face them.

He sent men through two different routes to lay siege to the abbey where the rebels were staying. Upon seeing the sturdy structure made of stone, William knew that siege equipment would be necessary to properly drive the men from hiding. Getting his army to the abbey had been difficult enough, but he sent for the equipment because he did not want to leave anything to chance.

The Anglo-Saxons saw how William was planning to attack, and knowing that they could not win under siege, they slipped away before William's siege could even begin. Without needing to initiate any actual fighting, William I had managed to win the battle, largely based on his reputation. By this point, his military prowess was well known around the island.

Those who had not managed to escape would face William's reputation and his brutal nature. Captured rebels were often blinded or mutilated, while others were placed in prison for the rest of their lives. Both Æthelwine and Morcar suffered cruel fates, though Morcar would survive and be released after outliving the Norman king. Waltheof, who became the earl of Northumbria in 1072, had a complicated relationship with the king, and this was not the first time where he had caused problems. However, William had ended up settling with the earl. Bizarrely enough, the king ended up giving his niece, Judith of Lens, to the earl in marriage. Waltheof is said to have been one of the last Anglo-Saxon earls, and he was executed under William's orders in 1076. Hereward managed to escape with some of his men, living to continue the rebellion elsewhere.

The actual fate of Hereward is unknown, though, as different sources provided different fates for the man. Some say that he was eventually killed by Norman soldiers. Others claim that he made peace with the king, with little details on exactly what kind of peace they were able to find, given how they both felt wronged by the other. Finally, some sources say that Hereward left the island entirely, living out the rest of his years on the continent.

Beyond the Rebellious Northern Anglo-Saxons

It appeared that William had finally gotten most of the north under his control, though it took him five long years to do so. However, he would soon find that the Anglo-Saxons who had resisted him had been a bit of a buffer to another long-standing enemy of the English—the Scottish.

Following the Norman conquest, the Scots had begun to allow the Anglo-Saxon rebels to live in the upper part of the island. King Malcolm III had been quick to find a way to continue to cause problems for whatever king was on the English throne by aiding and abetting his enemies. Military support was offered to the English rebels, particularly Edgar Ætheling. The king had married Edward the Confessor's niece (Edgar's sister), Margaret, giving him more of a stake in fighting against the Normans.

The Scots would constantly raid the area of Northumbria, but until 1072, William had not had a chance to face the Scottish king. It was all he could do to fight the forces to the south and the immediate north. With all of his other enemies finally out of the way, he turned his attention to the Scots. He was successful in stopping the raids and forcing Malcolm III to negotiate a peace agreement. As a part of that agreement, Edgar Ætheling (the man with the best claim to the throne) was forced into exile, spending the rest of his life in Flanders.

Atoning for the Conquest

Though he had managed to conquer the English, it is thought that William I felt some regret or that he at least desired to atone for what had happened that day at Hastings. Many men on both sides lost their lives over the course of the day. Around 1071, he had commissioned the construction of an abbey where the battle had been. It would seem that William I also had some respect for the king he had killed as he had ordered that the abbey's high altar be placed on the location where Harold II's body had been found after the battle had ended.

It is no longer scattered and stained with the bones and blood of those who fought in it, but the memories of the horrors of that day have lived until today, and it remains as one of the most well-known battles of the Middle Ages.

Though William had been successful in finally conquering the island, it had come at a high cost, both in money and in lives. It is unlikely that William had anticipated nearly as much resistance as he had faced, and his military prowess was tested in a way that it never would have been tested on the continent because of the strange island dynamics. The Battle of Hastings was likely the only time where William I could have been defeated, as Harold II was the only man with the experience and following that could have stopped him. Once William had defeated the king, it was mostly a matter of time before the rest of England would come under his reign.

Chapter 11 – The Domesday Book

William I spent about five years fighting a range of enemies. Between fighting the longtime enemies of the English and the English rebels who would not accept him, William spent a considerable amount of money ensuring that he had the army required to protect his claim as king. While he was willing to raid religious establishments, as well as taking from the Anglo-Saxon nobles to give to the Normans and others who had supported him during the initial invasion, this was not a sustainable method of funding an entire kingdom.

Toward the end of his reign, William I knew that he needed to set up a tax system to ensure that the Anglo-Saxons did not rise up and remove his lineage the way they had removed the Viking usurpers. The result was the Domesday Book.

Page from the Domesday Book

(Source: https://www.historic-uk.com/assets/Images/pagedomesdaybook.jpg?1390900110)

Commission of the Domesday Book

William's method of determining tax rates for his kingdom was based on a series of surveys that he commissioned in December of 1085. With nearly two decades between the time of his conquest and the time when he commissioned the survey, there was a question of which parts of the kingdom had recovered from his early methods to stamp out rebellions and which locations had prospered the most from his reign. The surveys were to result in a record of the status of the different regions, including both the cash and property wealth of his subjects.

Initial Assessment

Some data existed from earlier assessments, but there was no complete record of the status of each of the different regions. Since William had been so brutal in putting down rebellions, any records from before his conquest were likely obsolete anyway.

Royal commissioners were appointed to manage the surveys of the entire kingdom. At the time, the English counties stretched from the southern parts of the island to the Scottish border, which was at the Rivers Tees and Ribble. The commissioners were sent to the seven different regions, with three or four commissioners going to each region, and they were given a series of questions to ask the overlords and their subjects. Each county was to pick representatives who could speak to the status of the county and its assets.

According to the first account of the wealth of the different realms in William's kingdom, the commissioners identified 13,418 settlements. Each of the settlements, as determined by the commissioners, were compared to records that had been recorded earlier (both before the Norman conquest and since William's coronation). The findings were then entered in, giving a complete account of the wealth of those different counties. As was normal during the Middles Ages, the language used for official information like this was Latin, so the commissioners entered their data in a language that would likely be much easier for people to read today than if they had written it in Old English (Latin had not evolved since it was a dead language by the 11th century —it had become many different Italian dialects by this point). The Domesday Book was published in 1086, and it still exists today, though it is no longer updated now.

While it was meant as a way of determining the taxes of the region, what the Domesday Book does today is provide a unique look into the many different aspects of the kingdom that we would not have ordinarily gotten. The use of the lands was different across the kingdom, as well as the disputes that were currently causing problems for the landowners and their people. It provides a look at the lives of the people of the kingdom, something that is not available in nearly any other kingdom of the Middle Ages. For example, looking at the book today shows us what the most common means of raising money were in each of the districts and how much would have to be sold to pay the taxes levied on those areas.

Another interesting aspect that can be gleaned from the Domesday Book is that by the end of William I's reign, only four major English landowners had retained power. It is possible that William may have retained more of them had they not rebelled against him in the first five years. While he was certain to give away Anglo-Saxon lands to satisfy those who had supported his venture, many of the Anglo-Saxon nobles had perished at the Battle of Hastings. So, it is possible that he would not have had to take many lands from the remaining noble families. However, they proved to be difficult or flat-out refused to recognize his claim. Ultimately, William had to bring in more people from the continent to help him manage the kingdom. Men like Waltheof were few, and twenty years after the conquest, the Anglo-Saxon rulers were almost entirely removed from power, as shown by the Domesday Book.

Following its publication, many of those who reviewed the contents of the book felt that it was beyond what could have been expected, particularly given the number of lands and how diverse the means of making money were at the time. One person quipped that "there was no single hide nor a yard of land, nor indeed one ox nor one cow nor one pig which was left out." The lengthy account of the affairs, assets, and wealth of the settlements across the kingdom soon began to be compared with the Christian Last Judgment, which states that all Christian lives would be accounted for and judged upon their death. About one hundred years later, this comparison would result in the book being called the Domesday Book as a reference to the Last Judgment.

Despite the name, the records actually required two books to cover all of the data collected by the commissioners. The first volume is known as the Great Domesday, and it has data on all but three counties in the kingdom of 1086. The three absent counties are Essex, Norfolk, and Suffolk, which are included in the second volume, commonly referred to as the Little Domesday. It is unknown why these three counties were not summarized and added to the larger book. Combined, the books are 413 pages long, giving historians today an unprecedented look at the lives and state of the kingdom over nine centuries ago.

Chapter 12 – Effects of the Conquest

While the majority of the landowners and people controlling the regions may have been largely Norman, the people themselves were not replaced. England continued to be structured based on the traditions of the people. Over time, William I and the kings who followed him would begin to change that structure. Some people are under the impression that William I immediately implemented the changes, but it is far more likely that the changes to the different English systems were gradual. William I may not have learned much about the people that he believed he was promised to rule prior to Edward's death, but he did not appear to have intended to recreate Normandy in England. Given the problems that he had with the French king before his death, William may have seen the new lands as a way to start a kingdom according to his own methods. Remember, he had inherited Normandy as the bastard son of the previous lord, and he had become the new lord when he was still young. He had learned how to rule based on what others had established because of how young he was when he was placed in control.

While William was considerably different than previous kings (both Anglo-Saxon and Viking), he did take a greater interest in uniting the nation in a way that it had not been united in a long time. After all, his reign was preceded by questions of who the next rightful heir would be. The Vikings had continually taken control of the kingdom from the Anglo-Saxon over a century or so. Unlike William, though, they really had not replaced the people in charge, but they had reduced the influence of the prominent families or drove them into exile. Edward himself had been a victim of the constant changes in the crown, as he had spent most of his childhood and early adulthood in Normandy. William would finally give the nation of England a steady line of rulers with a more uniform method of ruling the people.

Changes to the Buildings and Records

One of the most obvious changes (looking at the structures built prior to the Norman conquest) is the building of structures, which were very different from what had existed on the island prior to William's arrival. The most notable change was in the number of castles that were built following the conquest. For the most part, Anglo-Saxons did not build castles, so there are few structures that could be classified as castles prior to 1066.

Initially, castles were made of wood, but the Normans soon began to build the more familiar stone castles that now dot much of the landscapes today. If you visit the United Kingdom today, many of the castle tours that you can take are only possible because of the events of October 14th, 1066.

In addition to the castles, William began to have cathedrals and abbeys improved and rebuilt to be larger. During this time, the architecture that was common across continental Europe began to appear across England. Even the churches attended by the common people often saw changes to make them more fashionable, at least according to the continental idea of fashion.

For all of the changes that were made under William, particularly architecture and law, it is thought that William I was likely illiterate, or that if he could read, he was not adept at it. Most of his life had been spent fighting for lands that were either rightfully his (as Normandy was after his father's death) or that he believed to be rightfully his. Because of these hardships, he had learned the importance of having records of events, whether they were land assessments or battles. This was one of the major reasons why there are so many records of his reign and how much the island nation had changed after the arrival of the Normans. That does not mean that the Anglo-Saxons did not keep records. We have their side of the story because of the annals they kept. However, they were not as rigorous in recording histories, as seen by the large gaps in events. The Normans made sure to write down nearly everything they thought was important, and that included how the government was to be run in the kingdom.

Old English was largely spoken by the people, while the Norman nobles largely spoke French. However, all government business was conducted and written in Latin, as seen in the Domesday Book. English and French were two drastically different languages, which made it difficult to communicate between the different classes. Latin was the one language that anyone who had any power or education would know. Even many of the common people would know basic Latin because it was used by priests during mass. As a language that was best understood by a majority of the people, Latin became the official language of the government. This still holds true today in English-speaking countries; their legal terms are all Latin, and many English-speaking nations use Latin in their governments (though principal documents are now written in English so that they can be understood by everyone, such as portions of the Magna Carta and the American Declaration of Independence and the US Constitution).

As seen with the creation of the Domesday Book, William I raised taxes on his people. By this point, most of the men in power were loyal to him, perhaps making this an easier action to take than it would have been had the Anglo-Saxon earls still been in power. The Norman lords had less land, which meant that their taxes were not as great as they would have been under the old division of the lands. However, it still was not a popular move. The king may not have faced rebellions because of the new taxes, but he did have some who resisted or lied to get out of paying as many taxes as they should have owed. The rise in taxes was easily justified as the first five years of constant rebellions and attacks from outsiders had been a huge strain on the Normans. William I's military strategies saw them eventually subdue their enemies, but to ensure that he could remain effective, he needed to have money, as well as loyalty. They still did not have a standing army, so William needed to be able to offer money to persuade people to leave their lands alone or to hire mercenaries when problems arose.

It is interesting to note that it was during this time that royal forests were first introduced. William I established royal forests, and they were ruled by their own set of laws. Perhaps the easiest correlation is how those forests would evolve by the time of Kings Richard I and John and the tales of Robin Hood. Only the nobility was allowed to hunt on these lands unless authorization was given to others to join them. It was just one more way to mark the difference between those in power and those who were not.

One tradition that the Normans brought with them from the continent was the idea of trial by battle. Problems between people of equal standing used to be settled through courts and negotiations. Under the Norman systems, a person in the higher classes of society could face an accuser in a trial by combat in order to determine who was in the right. In theory, the Christian god would settle the dispute because he would be on the side of the person who was right. Over time, trial by combat would lose some of the gravitas that it had when it was done as a way to settle legal disputes, as it instead became a way for people to settle pettier differences. These trials would devolve into duels over time.

Changes to the Elite, Society, and the Church

Because of the number of people who had chosen to fight the invaders than to submit to them, the change in power went well beyond just the people who were beside the king in his court. The changes also extended beyond just those who managed the different counties as well. Government officials were largely changed so that William knew he could trust them. This is likely why it was so easy for the changes to take effect more quickly than they otherwise would have.

The Church also saw a huge shift as the Anglo-Saxon church officials had largely sided with the English. Around the time of the Domesday Book's publication, only one of the fifteen bishops in the kingdom was English, while eleven were Normans. Three others had been brought in from different places around the continent.

With this change to the power dynamic in the country, the practice of giving lands in exchange for loyalty and services rendered to the king became far more common, which was a practice that was not nearly as prominent before the arrival of the Normans. Prior to William's arrival, the Anglo-Saxons had determined how much service they were required to give the king (including military aid) based on the lands that they owned. As seen with Harold Godwinson following his father's death, earls were not allowed to have too much land as it would cause an imbalance in power. Under the Norman power structure, though, a person could continue to increase their lands and power, just as William had done as a young man when he consolidated power in and around Normandy.

As a direct result of a loyal family being able to gain more lands from the king, the family dynamics began to change. Nobles were now able to gain land through inheritance and conquest, and lands could be divided among several heirs instead of them passing down to one person. This created more tension in some families, particularly as some sons were excluded, but it tightened the bonds of others.

By putting people who were loyal to him in all of the major positions of power, both secular and religious, William was able to enact changes that likely would not have been possible had he been faced with the Anglo-Saxon earls. They were accustomed to autonomy, which would have made it more difficult for William to enact these changes.

The constant rebellions by the Anglo-Saxons also meant that the earldoms were reduced in size to better ensure that problems were easier to manage. Small earldoms meant that William I could offer more lands to his loyal followers, but it also meant that the new earls would have to continue to work hard to gain more power and influence. This made the power dynamic more geared toward a hierarchy that would keep the king on top and the nobles fighting among themselves to gain power and influence (instead of directly challenging the king).

The Domesday Book helped to show just how much contention there was among the people, so it was clear that a different type of court system was needed for the Normans. Called the Lords, the new courts were held by the lords of the respective lands. This began an integration of the continental feudal system in Britain because the lords of different lands would determine how a dispute would be settled. This also brought an interesting change to how a murder was resolved. The Normans reintroduced murdrum fines, which the Danes had originally introduced. These fines only applied if a Norman descendant was murdered. Should the killer fail to be identified, then the entire English community would be required to pay a fine to compensate the Norman family for the murder of their family member. While this clearly shows just how much opposition the Normans faced in the early days of William's reign, it set up a dynamic that would become incredibly problematic over the centuries. Even after the lines of inheritance were established and the difference between the Normans and the Anglo-Saxons shrunk, more importance was placed on the life of the people in power.

With an emphasis on the people in power and a shift in how lands were divided among them, the number of people who were free decreased. People who had worked the lands for themselves under the Anglo-Saxon system opted to work the lands of landlords because it was easier to be under their rule than to try to survive as they had under the old system.

William I is not generally thought of as a pious man today, but there was a marked increase in the number of monasteries in England during his reign. It is certainly an interesting dichotomy since he would also raid them for funds to keep his military funded when needed. Perhaps it was out of a sense of guilt for these transgressions that he increased the number of religious facilities. As he took lands from the Anglo-Saxons and shrunk the amount of land he gave to his loyal subjects, William kept some of the lands separate. These lands he gave to the continental monasteries, which resulted in more of them being built. It is also possible that he was trying to curry favor with the pope, who had sided with him and his claim to the English throne.

Changes in Relationships with the Continent

The Anglo-Saxons had a long and contentious relationship with the Vikings, but they had much tighter bonds with them as well. England and France did not have as deep a connection, despite the number of English nobles who fled to Normandy following the Viking conquests. However, with the Normans taking over the largest kingdom on the island, the ties that had largely bound the British and the Scandinavian countries were largely severed. Instead of the close, familial relationships that they had maintained, with many British and Scandinavian elite marrying, the bonds would be forged with the French elite instead. There would never again be a serious threat of the Scandinavian countries trying to claim the English crown.

Ironically, this would later prove to be a source of serious contention between England and France, as the claim over the French throne by an English noble would be much stronger than the claim that William I had over England. The Norman conquest is one of the reasons for both the formation of the Angevin Empire and later the Hundred Years' War, where the person with the greatest claim to the French throne was actually the English king.

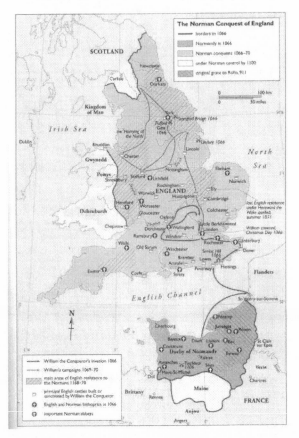

William of Normandy's Lands after the Norman Conquest

(*Source: https://www.awesomestories.com/asset/view/William-the-Conquerer-Invasion-Map*)

A Significant Change to the Language

There are few languages that are as diverse today as they were around 1,000 years ago, but English is a notable exception. The linear evolution of most languages makes it easy to classify them as being Germanic or Romantic because the lands around the continent largely remained under the control of people who had similar languages.

England was unique in that it was under the influence of so many different languages from the time the Romans arrived. The influence of the Roman invaders can be seen in some of the older roots of the language, but most of it was removed following their departure, as the Anglo-Saxons began to resume their own traditions.

Next, the Vikings would spend several centuries raiding and then settling among the native peoples. The influence of their language is more obvious, as English is largely considered to be a Germanic language.

However, the biggest change to the English language was a direct result of the Norman invasion. Once William I became king, the primary language used by his court was the language that he spoke—French. Though it was primarily used by those of Norman descent, French was also used by some of the nobility and others of English descent, which, over time, blended with the native tongue, changing it enough that a native English speaker today cannot hope to understand the language spoken around the time of the Norman invasion.

An Interesting Note on the Norman Lineage and Previous Kings

The subjugation of the Anglo-Saxons was so complete that the Normans largely ignored the accomplishments of the kings before them. The best illustration of this desire to ignore Britain's prior history and the dubious claim of William I was in the way his descendants would look at kings who reigned before him. According to William's reasoning, he was the heir to Edward the Confessor, and without Edward's promise of the throne, William would not have had any claim that could be backed by the Normans or the Church. This should have meant that Edward would have been called King Edward I. However, he is always called simply King Edward or, more often, Edward the Confessor. This is because King Edward I was a king of Norman descent. In numbering the kings of the same name, they literally ignored the prior Anglo-Saxon king. This gave more importance to the king of Norman descent and showed a complete break between the Anglo-Saxon period and the Norman rule.

To some extent, the desire to ignore the history of the Anglo-Saxons showed an understanding on the Norman part that their claim was not legitimate. William had not come to power peacefully, and with as many years of resistance as the Normans had faced, it had to have been clear on some level to them that they were invaders, like the Vikings before them. They had just been more successful in usurping and keeping the throne. Harold II was perhaps not the rightful heir either, but his rule would not have seen a complete shift in how the kingdom was run. It is also possible that this denial of the Anglo-Saxon kings before him was in retaliation for the reception William had among his new subjects. As the English had rejected him and his claim, the Normans rejected their place in their own history.

Chapter 13 –Records of 1066 CE – Insight into a Time of Turmoil

While there is little known about most events 950 years ago, historians have a surprising amount of information about the events of 1066. It was certainly a turning point in history, but it would be expected that there would be far more of a one-sided account of what exactly happened. Instead, we have a fairly lengthy record of the events from both the Norman side and the Anglo-Saxon side. This is in large part because the Anglo-Saxons still constituted a majority of the population. The Normans may have started to claim the higher positions in government, but the Anglo-Saxons already had their own means of recording the events of their time.

The Bayeux Tapestry

The Norman version of events, including William's claim to the throne, is recorded on a 230-foot-long piece of cloth called the Bayeux Tapestry. In total, there are 75 scenes depicted on the tapestry, though it was originally longer. The end of this unique piece of art has been missing, though it is not known when this part of the tapestry was removed or why it was removed. It has led to some interesting discussions among academics about what part of history was exactly lost. We may not be able to say for certain what the last scenes were, but many people believe that it was likely a depiction of William being crowned as the new king.

The name Bayeux Tapestry is not strictly accurate as the images were not woven into the cloth, which is how tapestries are made. Instead, the scenes were embroidered onto a long piece of linen. It is estimated that the work was completed in 1070. Since it was made by the generation after the defeat of the English, it is considered to be a fairly reliable account of how the Normans viewed the events leading up to the battle. It is also believed that the Bishop of Bayeux, Odo, William's half-brother, was the one who commissioned the work. If this is true, it almost certainly depicts the events as William would have seen them, as Odo would have heard William's perspective. However, it is also possible that it has a slant because of a desire to strengthen the family's claim to the throne.

It is unfortunate that we don't know who completed this impressive needlework, as the person or persons who were the artists behind it was not recorded. It was the Anglo-Saxons who were considered the most adept at needlework in Europe, which meant that the artists were very likely Anglo-Saxons. Some speculate that the scenes depicted on the cloth were actually recorded from depictions that were in manuscripts that were located in Canterbury at the time.

The cloth reads like a book, starting on the left side and moving to the right. There are many scenes that appear to be inspired by the methods of recording histories on scrolls. This presents the events in more of a historical context, like a record instead of simply as a work of art. However, given the subject matter (the history of events leading up to the Battle of Hastings), it provides a record of more than just the main events leading up to the battle. In this sense, it is comparable more to a work of fiction or myth since it gives the viewer a look into the details of daily life as they take in the events beings depicted.

The Bayeux Tapestry provides a lot more than just a look at the events that resulted in the Norman conquest of England. With 75 scenes, it provides a lot of context about the lives of the Norman people during the 11th century, or at least the lives of the nobles and their servants. Some scenes that might appear mundane are included, such as large dinners, the types of food they ate, and how they dressed (including servants). It goes on to depict a war council as they plan for how they will attack. There are also depictions of the way they prepared for the war. These scenes provide some hints as to what they wore when they went into battle as well. The tactics used by William the Conqueror highlight his use of the cavalry to scatter Harold II's infantry. Based on this, some think that the Normans were accustomed to using cavalry during battle and that much of their success could have come from their skill on horseback.

The cloth may be an elegant depiction of the Norman perspective, but it was most likely created by Anglo-Saxon artisans. This makes it one of the first examples of Anglo-Norman art, which would evolve over the next few decades.

Scene from the Bayeux Tapestry: William of Normandy Learns about King Edward's Death and Harold II's Coronation

(*Source:*
https://en.wikipedia.org/wiki/File:Tapisserie_agriculture.JPG)

The *Anglo-Saxon Chronicle*

The *Anglo-Saxon Chronicle* is a recording of several centuries of British history, starting from the reign of King Alfred the Great in 871 CE and ending around 1154 CE, nearly a century after the Norman invasion. Unlike the Bayeux Tapestry, the chronicles are multiple works of writing. It is unknown how many have been written, but six manuscripts remain intact today. A seventh managed to survive to the modern period, but it was destroyed sometime during the 18th century.

The remaining manuscripts are designated by letters, with A being the oldest manuscript. Each copy of the manuscripts was stored in separate locations, so they do not contain all of the same information, but there is a lot of overlap in what they detail. Naturally, all of the manuscripts are recorded in Old English or Anglo-Saxon, which makes them totally inaccessible to modern-day English speakers.

Around the time of the Norman conquest, the English language began to significantly change as Normans began to integrate with the Anglo-Saxons over time. One of the manuscripts was also translated into Latin, making it more accessible to people over the years.

These chronicles are the oldest recording of any European country written in a native tongue instead of in Latin. With several hundred years recorded in these manuscripts, there are many notable events that signaled important changes on the island over the years. The Battle of Hastings is described and notes how King Harold II fought bravely despite the obvious disadvantages. It is through the *Anglo-Saxon Chronicle* that we know that Harold and two of his loyal brothers were killed that day.

All of the information recorded on the manuscripts that still survive today provides a unique look at history that is not available in nearly any other country. We are able to see several different perspectives because no single manuscript was written by just one person. They do provide biased versions of events, but they are from an angle that is more from the common person's point of view (or at least the clerics who would have tended the common people). Like the Bayeux Tapestry, the *Anglo-Saxon Chronicle* offers a look into more than just a single event, as each event covered offers details surrounding it.

What is particularly interesting about the tapestry and the *Anglo-Saxon Chronicle* is that the information they provide is reflected in each other. This is perhaps why the battle is still so well known today.

Anglo-Saxon Chronicle – Single Winchester Page of the Manuscript

(Source: https://en.wikipedia.org/wiki/File:ASC_Parker_page.png)

Conclusion

The Romans were the first recorded people to have successfully invaded the nations on the island that would one day become England, Wales, and Scotland. Not long after they left the island, the Vikings began to attack. Unlike the Romans, the Vikings would largely integrate with the people of Britain. To fight the stream of Viking invaders who had no interest in turning the island into a home, the Anglo-Saxons rose up.

With the ebb and flow of power, there was a constant question of succession. The Vikings who managed to take the Anglo-Saxon throne were considered pretenders. But what really made the succession of the English throne difficult was that royalty would frequently intermarry (something that happened throughout Europe, which made the question of succession a constant problem elsewhere as well), so even if there was not a claim to the throne by blood, many rulers could claim it through marriage. The short period where the Anglo-Saxons retook the throne ended not long after King Æthelred II was restored and then suddenly died. Though he had children by his first wife, his second wife, Emma of Normandy, was far more assertive and found a way to keep the throne by marrying King Cnut, a Viking who had invaded and claimed the throne for himself. It was from this that the question of succession would become muddled a couple of decades later. Eventually, her son, Edward, would achieve the throne (though he was not the son she had wanted to ascend it). He only achieved the crown by agreeing to the terms set by the Anglo-Saxons, particularly Godwin.

When King Edward the Confessor died without any children, the kingdom fell back into the quagmire of determining succession. As Edward had made vague promises of succession throughout most of his life, there were several people who felt they were entitled to the throne, most notably William the Bastard, the ruler of Normandy. When Harold Godwinson was quickly coronated as the new king, William felt that his throne had been stolen.

While William planned to invade, another man who felt he had a claim to the throne, King Harald Hardrada of Norway, attacked in the north. King Harold II had no sooner defeated him than William arrived in the south. The Battle of Hastings would see the death of King Harold and the end of the Anglo-Saxon period.

William the Bastard became known as William the Conqueror, and under his reign, England began to change. From the social structure and the way the government ran to the language itself, the island nation began to more closely resemble the continental countries.

Though William ultimately became king, two very different accounts of the events leading up to the Battle of Hastings have come down through the ages: the Bayeux Tapestry and the *Anglo-Saxon Chronicle*. It gives historians a better look at the factions and ideas of the conqueror and the conquered, something that we seldom get to see following a successful invasion of any nation or kingdom. This has made it easier to get a more well-rounded understanding of the different perspectives and shows a historic transition of a nation that would one day be one of the largest empires in the world.

Here's another book by Captivating History you might be interested in

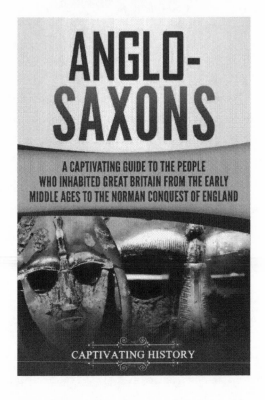

Bibliography

10 Facts about the Battle of Hastings, Sally Coffey, 2019, The Official Magazine Britain, Chelsea Magazine Co, www.britain-magazine.com/

1066 and the Norman Conquest, English Heritage, 2019, www.english-heritage.org.uk/

1066: A Timeline of the Norman Conquest, Peter Konieczny, October 8, 2017, Medieval Warfare, Karwansaray Publishers, www.karwansaraypublishers.com.

A History of the Norman Conquest of 1066, Robert Wilde, April 7, 2017, Thought Co., www.thoughtco.com

Alfred the Great (849 AD – 899 AD), BBC: History, http://www.bbc.co.uk/history.

Alfred: King of Wessex, Dorothy Whitelock, Encyclopedia Britannica, last edited January 1, 2019, www.britannica.com.

Anglo-Saxon Chronical, Editors of Encyclopedia Britannica, 2019, www.britannica.com

Before the Norman Conquest, A History of the County of York: The City of York, ed. P M Tillott (London, 1961), pp. 2-24. British History Online www.british-history.ac.uk/ 4 October 2019.

Harold Godwinson, Mark Cartwright, January 14, 2019, Ancient History Encyclopedia, www.ancient.eu

Harold II (Godwineson) (c.1020 – 1066), 2014, BBC, www.bbc.co.uk/history

History: Norman Britain, Neil McIntosh, November 6, 2014, BBC, www.bbc.co.uk/history.

Overview: The Vikings, 800 to 1066, Professor Edward James, March 29, 2011, History, BBC, www.bbc.co.uk/history.

Robert I, Duke of Normandy, Editors of Britannica, 2019, www.britannica.com

The Anglo-Saxon Chronical, 2004, English Monarchs, Saxon Index, www.englishmonarchs.co

The Art of Conquest in England and Normandy, Dr. Diane Reilly, October 4, 2019, Khan Academy, www.khanacademy.org.

The Battle of Hastings, Return to Anglo-Saxon England, 2019, penelope.uchicago.edu/

The Bayeux Tapestry, Dr. Kristine Tanton, October 4, 2019, Khan Academy, www.khanacademy.org.

The Domesday Book, Ben Johnson, 2019, Historic UK, www.historic-uk.com/

The History Files :Part 1: Western Decline, Peter Kessler, June 30, 2007, The History Files, Kessler Associates, www.historyfiles.co.uk/.

The Impact of the Norman Conquest of England, Mark Cartwright, January 23, 2019, Ancient History Encyclopedia, www.ancient.eu/.

The Incredible Life of Harald Hardrada: The Last of the 'Great Vikings, Dattaterya Mandal, September 5, 2015, Realm of History, www.realmofhistory.com/

The Norman Invasion of 1066 CE, Western Civilization, October 4, 2019, OER Services, courses.lumenlearning.com.

The Roman 'Brexit': how life in Britain Changed after 409AD, Will Bowden, 2019, University of Nottingham, The Conversation US Inc, theconversation.com.

The Romans in England, Ben Johnson, 2019, Historic UK Ltd, www.historic-uk.com/.

William I 'The Conqueror' (r.1066-1087), 2019, The Royal Household, Crown, www.royal.uk/william-the-conqueror

Made in the USA
Middletown, DE
20 June 2021

42797030R00071